INTO THE WEEDS

INTO THE WEEDS

LYDIA DAVIS

THE 2024 WINDHAM-CAMPBELL LECTURE

YALE UNIVERSITY PRESS
NEW HAVEN AND LONDON

The *Why I Write* series is published with assistance from the
Windham-Campbell Literature Prizes, which are administered by
the Beinecke Rare Book and Manuscript Library at Yale University.

"When We Are Dead and Gone" and "Improving My German" reprinted by
permission from OUR STRANGERS by Lydia Davis (New York: Bookshop
Editions, 2023).

Excerpt from "As You Came from the Holy Land," copyright © 1973 by John
Ashbery. Originally appeared in "Poetry"; from SELF-PORTRAIT IN A CONVEX
MIRROR (1977, 2007) by John Ashbery. Used by permission of Viking Books, an
imprint of Penguin Publishing Group, a division of Penguin Random House LLC;
and Carcanet Press, UK. All rights reserved.

"Flaubert and Point of View" from CAN'T AND WON'T: STORIES by
Lydia Davis. Copyright © 2014 by Lydia Davis. Reprinted by permission
of Farrar, Straus and Giroux. All Rights Reserved.

Yale University Press books may be purchased in quantity for educational, business,
or promotional use. For information, please e-mail sales.press@yale.edu
(U.S. office) or sales@yaleup.co.uk (U.K. office).

Set in Yale and News Gothic BT type.
Printed in the United States of America.

Library of Congress Control Number: 2025936907

ISBN 978-0-300-27974-0 (hardcover)

A catalogue record for this book is available from the British Library.

Authorized Representative in the EU: Easy Access System Europe,
Mustamäe tee 50, 10621 Tallinn, Estonia, gpsr.requests@easproject.com

10 9 8 7 6 5 4 3 2 1

INTO THE WEEDS

When, late last winter, I began thinking about how to approach writing about why I write, as I had been invited to do the previous fall, I was reading a book I had been given for Christmas called *The Wheelwright's Shop*. This led me to ask a different question first — why other writers write and, specifically, why certain other writers write and, more specifically, why they wrote certain of their books and, most specifically, why George Sturt had written this book. My pondering the motives of other writers, however, may be pure speculation — or fairly pure speculation, since sometimes you at least know why they *think* they write something, or *say* they write something.

When I was invited, last fall, I wanted to be willing to set out to talk about my writing, but I found that

I was thinking about reading—reading the writing of someone else. I do so much reading, I am so often in the company of other writers, and contending with how they write. My reading is my reaction to the writing of other people. I may think that my reading, or anyone's reading, completes their writing. They write something and then I either read it with pleasure, or read it without pleasure, or decide not to continue reading it. Or I don't even open the book.

When I was invited, last fall, to write on this topic, I agreed. But the subject proposed is difficult. I drew a blank, although I do have a lot to say, generally speaking.

A person once said to me, "You're a writer. You must have a lot to say." He was making an assumption. I've thought about his assumption many times. Is it that simple? Do I write because I have a lot to say? I do have a lot to say. No matter how much I have said, isn't there always more to say? But then, I imagine everyone has a lot to say, writers and nonwriters alike. I can't imagine anyone not having a lot to say—even if they keep their mouth closed.

Human beings with a lot to say like to make noise. So do crickets, dogs, mice, other insects, rabbits when frightened or being killed, moose, and many, many others. It is impressive to think of all the creatures on earth and all the different noises they make, for different reasons. Some of their noises are effective. Some fail to have an effect.

When John Ashbery was invited to deliver the six Charles Eliot Norton Lectures at Harvard, some ten years before the turn of the millennium, he surmised that he was being asked to explain his own poetry, which he knew was reputed to be hermetic. But, as he explained in the first Norton lecture, he felt that his poetry *was* the explanation. "The explanation of what?" he asked. "Of my thought, whatever that is." He chose not to try to explain his own poetry, and quoted John Barth, who said, "You shouldn't pay very much attention to anything writers say. They don't know why they do what they do." (In fact, that could be my epigraph for this essay.) And instead, he devoted the six lectures to six "certifiably minor" poets who, though far from the only poets who had influenced him, were among the ones he read "to get started; a poetic jump-start."

I had a stimulating and peaceful long afternoon riding a bus west from Boston to Pittsfield, Massachusetts, with only a few stops along the way and only a few other, quiet passengers, reading the book that eventually resulted from Ashbery's lectures: *Other Traditions.* It was thoughtful and clearly reasoned and judiciously illustrated with quoted lines from the poets — just enough from each poet — and Ashbery's analysis of one poet after another was enlightening. It was the perfect book to read on a public bus, a quiet one. Because the book demanded attention, it was suited to efforts of close, concentrated, but intermittent attention, and at the same time, if I paused in my reading and thinking, the steady forward motion of the bus included me in something that continued to happen even when I stopped reading. I would read a portion of a page and then look up to think about it, gazing out at a landscape that was fairly monotonous, just monotonous enough not to distract me — the woods and more woods and occasional fields and occasional houses and barns and one broad river and one steep climb to a mountaintop and one descent therefrom and along the way at some point the topiary sign spelling out "Friendly's." This was the Massachusetts Turnpike, already familiar to me from other trips.

What a sensible idea of Ashbery's, I thought, and modest — to direct attention away from himself. It also worked to his own benefit—he was more interested in exploring these other poets and articulating his exploration than he was in repeating his ideas about himself, if he would admit to any. It can also be dangerous to look too closely into the magic that produces something you write. Barth: Writers don't know why they do what they do . . .

After I have been asked why I write, and as I am attempting to answer that question, the word *bother* becomes relevant in a particular sense, though I was not conscious of it in just that sense one year ago, before I read what I read recently.

The word *bother* came into my life in a specific, positive sense when I read an interview given by John Ashbery in which he talked about how he encountered the source of his long poem "Self-Portrait in a Convex Mirror" and its title.

It is not that John Ashbery is always my highest or most useful example for things, it is more a matter of chance, in this case. This essay that I am writing, or attempting to write, in answer to the question of why I write, gets written in real time, and things happen during that time. During that time, the book group I am part of chose to read Ashbery's collection of poems *Self-Portrait in a Convex Mirror.* All of us had read it before, but when you reach your sixties and seventies, as we have, a book you can truthfully say you have read may actually have been read by you so long ago that it is as though not read. For this meeting we planned to read the title poem, which is long, together with whichever other poems interested each of us. In intervals between continuing to read the title poem, which I found dense and hard to understand, I was thinking about a title I associate with Ashbery, "Peter and Mother," which I often think of, even though it may not be the title of any poem of his. Because I wasn't sure it was the title of a poem of his, rather than, say, the title of an article about him, I searched the internet for it and instead found a 2015 interview with him by Adam Fitzgerald in the magazine and on the website *Interview.*

What I found, in reading the interview, were some comments he made about titling his poems but also, along the way, two or even three possible answers to why he wrote. About the titles of his poems, he simply said, "They come to me."

The first thing he said was that he first encountered the painting by the young Francesco Parmigianino titled *Self-Portrait in a Convex Mirror* in the form of a reproduction in a literary magazine and that he was "immediately grabbed and bothered" by the painting and thought he would like to "do something" with it. But he did nothing at the time. Many years later he happened to see the painting itself in a museum in Vienna. He says, "And that did it. I knew I had to do something about it then." And he uses the word *bother* in this way, in this interview, about at least one other thing that inspired a poem.

The formulation "do something about it" is a blunt and truthful way of expressing your response to material that "bothers" you—in a good way—when you encounter it.

I encountered the Ashbery interview when I was beginning to struggle to answer the question of why I write. Here is a very concise and truthful answer: the reason I write a particular story may be because something—which I call "material," as in "raw material"—bothers me until I "do something" about it. In these cases, "bother" is wholly positive. The beauty of the black cows across the road, the geometry of the positions they adopted, bothered me in that way, and the shadow of a grain of salt on a counter bothered me one late afternoon.

I think of the phrase "Peter and Mother" — more often than anyone might imagine — because I like the way it sounds and yet it is awkward.

Some of the pieces of language that persist in my memory are ones that seem stylistically awkward or faulty. One is Ashbery's (or not Ashbery's) title "Peter and Mother." Another is Shakespeare's "When yellow leaves, or none, or few, do hang / Upon those boughs . . ." Which I can hear also as the first notes of the musical scale sung out of order: "mi, or do, or re." Yet another, which I hear as redundant, I remember from *Moby-Dick* but is quoted by Melville from the book of Job: "And I only am escaped alone to tell thee." (Though the escape is only temporary.) (In the first, British edition of the novel, the epilogue in which Ishmael speaks this sentence was mistakenly omitted. And so it appeared to readers that Ishmael had drowned along with the others — and if so, how could he be telling this story?)

Three of the five in my original talkative family are gone, their voices and thoughts permanently silenced now, except on paper in various places in this house, and the other one besides me left alive is declining — as I am inevitably, too, though at a different rate and from different causes. Either he or I will be the only one left, eventually, who can bear witness to the life of that particular family, (temporarily) "escaped alone to tell thee."

Another wrong order that is perfectly good, in the sentence where it sits, is Flaubert's "She closed the door behind him, when he left, with a feeling of satisfaction that surprised even her" — speaking of Emma Bovary and her father, whose company during his visit had irritated her. I, when a teacher of writing, though I was not overly didactic or rule-bound, used to advise the young writers to tell the actions *in the order* in which they happened. But in this case, Flaubert is achieving a sly emphasis, whether he meant to or not: Emma closes the door on her father even before he is out the door!

My translating life is more or less over now. But after I finished *Madame Bovary,* the last novel I translated, I was not yet through with translating. I went on to translate a number of very short stories, which I could accomplish in a day or two, if not a couple of hours (rough draft). And I had a feeling similar to Ashbery's "do something about it" in the case of these short works. When I read the very short stories of A. L. Snijders in Dutch and some years later of Peter Bichsel in German and after that a few by Gunnhild Øyehaug in Norwegian (Nynorsk), they captivated me and I wanted to "do something" about them—in this case, translate them. I was not content simply to read them as best I could and move on. I wanted to remake them for myself, in English.

The second helpful thing Ashbery says is in answer to Fitzgerald's question about how he reacts to his own work when he rereads it: "I frequently like [my work] very much when I do read it. When I come across it, maybe it's in a desk drawer or somewhere, and it's some poem you wrote and have completely forgotten about. When you read it, you're thinking it was written by someone else. It's this sort of feeling of ecstasy that can be supplied by nothing else. Maybe that's why one writes."

This divorce from oneself—this feeling of distance or estrangement from one's own writing—is in concrete and permanent form described in an account that I was told or that I read about George Oppen as he was suffering from the early stages of dementia. He was walking around a room in his house reading his own poems, which had been framed and hung on the wall—I may have this somewhat inaccurate, but the gist is correct— walking from one to another, reading them, in a room at home, and observing to whoever was there witnessing this that he found them to be quite good, not knowing the poems were his own. Although he did not know they were his, he clearly felt a compatibility with them. They were poems he liked and would have been glad to have written.

The process of writing, or this kind of process of writing, anyway, that I'm considering here, includes something outside oneself. It is something outside myself that comes to take hold of me and in a sense use me as an instrument to come into being. I am instrumental. I am not making something up myself, out of myself. Something outside me is being given, or offered, to me, by chance. I then concentrate on it, give it shape, and in the process open myself to developments in the material that seem to come of their own volition. This openness to involuntary developments is what is most endangered by a knock on my study door at the wrong time, though strangely less endangered by the ongoing hubbub that may surround me on a crowded train or in a bar or café, because no one knows me there and even a momentary intrusion is likely to be impersonal and undisturbing. ("Can you please move your coat?")

Ashbery experienced, he said, "ecstasy" at reading a poem of his own that he liked.

When I began trying in all honesty to answer the question of why I write, one of the first answers I came to was for the pleasure of it. There is, for me, at least, pleasure at each stage of the writing. There is the initial impulse, the recognition of the potential richness of the material—got to "do something" about that. And then the forming of that original provocative material into something that, it seems to me at the moment, couldn't have any other or better form, working at the form until it seems to fit perfectly what the material asks for. And then, later, the tension past, eventually, no hurry, the sharing of the finished piece, seeing it printed, or, still later, going back and reading it again—usually for some practical reason, or else just because I opened to that page. Or reading it aloud and enjoying someone else's enjoyment—we relish together what that original material turned into.

But it may be more accurate to say that at the beginning of the process is emotion — though often that emotion is pleasure.

Something that was *not* a reason I started writing in the first place was for fame or money.

But I may have thought, as a twenty-year-old, that one wrote to convey a message, as in a *serious poem*. But I soon stopped thinking I needed to convey a message, or even have a message. I had some messages inside me then, and I still have plenty of messages inside me, but not to convey explicitly or even implicitly in writing, except involuntarily, maybe only in rants or harangues out loud to people. People who would rather I quieted down.

I don't write to convey a message, and I don't write stories to achieve any particular purpose, I don't write stories to persuade a reader of something I believe, though I have many, many beliefs.

I don't write a story for any particular audience, I don't think of a reader as I am writing it, though after I've finished writing it, I am glad, or touched, if a person enjoys it or is moved by it.

I don't write a story to move someone, though someone may be moved. It is not that direct. It is more indirect than that: I encounter something that moves me, I let a story evolve from it, or I guide the material into the form of a story that fits it, that suits the power or beauty of that original material. Then a reader reads the story, and if that reader is of a certain temperament not too unlike mine in one or several respects, for instance, having a similar sense of humor, or any sense of humor at all, he or she may be moved by the story. But moved, I could say, only, in a sense, by my story as *intermediary*, as conveying what was inherent, for me, as I saw it, or possible, in the original material.

When I think about that twenty-year-old searching for a serious topic — where was it? — for her to-be-serious poem, I believe she actually admired good poems she had read and wanted to write a poem as good. Later, when I was no longer trying to write good poems, but trying to write good stories, I probably wanted to write prose as eccentric and distinct and clear and insistent as Samuel Beckett's and would copy out sentences from Beckett and study them.

John Clare said, in a poem, that he found his poems "in the fields" and "only wrote them down." This is not exactly what happens for me — and it probably did not for him—but my experience is that a piece of writing starts with something outside coming in. I write something because it occurs to me to write it—*it* occurs to *me*, rather than that *I* go out in search of *it*. Going out in search of a suitable topic is something I did early on, when I thought, as a twenty-year-old wanting to write "poetry," that a poem should be serious and have a serious subject, so I should search my mind and experience for a serious subject and then write about it.

I think it is all right, in the beginning, to want to write "poetry" and to think a poem should be serious. It is a starting point. Later, things will reverse direction, and it will be the poem, or at least the raw material for the poem, that comes to you wanting to be written.

I don't really see a poem as an animated creature asking to come to me, but Russell Edson, whose stories I found crucially liberating when I first encountered them in my twenties and whose imagination was wild, and domestic, and uninhibited, and open to considering the cruelty of family relations, and open to impossible situations, and open to inanimate things being demanding, and who tended to anthropomorphize things, including structural parts of a house, turned a poem into an animated creature in one of his stories, "New Prose about an Old Poem." (I say he wrote stories, but he said he wrote poems.) This little story is about a poem that is too good to throw away but not good enough to publish. The poem is carried away by the wind and the poet is relieved because he won't have to continue reconsidering it every now and then. But then the wind returns it to his desk. "The poem is glad to be home, and wants to be read again." The poet thinks he might send it out in the mail — submit it for publication — but knows he won't and says he "will have to go on being nice to it for the rest of his life." He is dramatizing the situation of a writer's having a folder or a drawer full of drafts that are not hopeless but not finished or really good, either — a locked or paralyzed situation. Most writers have these folders or drawers.

Stories come to me of their own accord, that is the usual way it works, but I have sometimes been goaded to write something by a request coming from outside.

This past spring, I experienced complete darkness one evening, the kind that people describe as not being able to see your hand before your face, as I left a building on a rural road with only darkened, thus invisible, houses nearby. A few weeks later, I was asked by a magazine if I would write about an "object of desire." At the time they asked me, I had something I wanted to write about — that experience of unexpected total darkness that had so startled me. I decided that would be my object of desire — total darkness being a thing so rare in our brightly illuminated world.

It was in fact through an earlier interest in darkness that I had first come to read the Surrey wheelwright George Sturt, not through my friend's gift; my friend's choice of this author for me as his yearly gift was coincidental and came as quite a surprise on that sunny Christmas afternoon.

I was interested in darkness, night, and sleep long before I was asked to write about an object of desire because of a long-planned project of mine that I have still not given up, even though I began planning it more than thirty years ago. Either I will return to it and complete it, or it will be in one of the folders or boxes I finally leave behind. George Steiner wrote a book about all the projects he never completed — *My Unwritten Books.* This is a book that attracts me and that I may one day have to write, too.

The project was not fiction. I was intending to expand upon an existing study by a French historian of a village in the south of France as it was in the early fourteenth century, when a full moon was so bright, or really — since the moon itself was no brighter than it is now — the air was so clear that one could go outside on a night of full moon and read a page by its light, and when the villagers I was studying would regularly refer to a certain time of the night as the time of their "second sleep." I did not know what this second sleep was, so I bought a book called *At Day's Close: Night in Times Past,* by A. Roger Ekirch, about nighttime and nighttime habits through the ages, that did explain it. From earliest times, when there was no electricity, no oil or kerosene lamps, only firelight and sometimes candles or torches, moon and stars, the natural pattern of nighttime sleep was this: to sleep from evening or later for about four hours until midnight or after, then to wake spontaneously and be up for an hour or so, tending the fire, checking on the children or the animals, smoking a pipe, talking by the fireside, reading (by moonlight or firelight), or even visiting with neighbors — or going out to commit a crime — and then to sleep again for another four hours or so, for one's second sleep, till morning.

After I was asked to write about an object of desire and began writing about darkness, I remembered another passage I had read in *At Day's Close* in which George Sturt—though I did not remember his name then—was quoted speaking of the utter darkness of the night in his English village when he was a young man, before the turn of the twentieth century—so dark, on some nights, that one knew where the road was only from one's familiarity with the feel of its dips and rises underfoot, and might, if one was not carrying a candle, bump face-to-face straight into another person coming the other way. I had wanted to read the book by Sturt from which the quote was taken, so I acquired it—it was not *The Wheelwright's Shop* but *Change in the Village,* which he wrote under a pseudonym, George Bourne—to protect his local reputation as a wheelwright!

But there is an evocation of darkness in *The Wheelwright's Shop* as well. As Sturt tells us, when the wheel-maker George Cook was done for the day, he would walk home alone (because he was deaf, Sturt says). At home, he had a donkey and donkey cart, probably a pig (Sturt isn't sure), a garden, a patch of hops, a hop dryer, and elderberry bushes to supply berries for wine. For a time, Cook had eye trouble and had to stay home. Sturt used to walk over to his cottage once a week or so to see how he was doing. This is where, in the book, darkness is described again: "The walk out of Farnham up the hill into the night, then down the steeper hill under the pitchy darkness of Culverlands trees into the all but unknown murk of Compton . . . found its goal when at last the cottage door was opened and, momentarily dazzled, I was let in from the night to the little warm-lit living room." There he would be given some homemade elderberry wine to warm him up.

Note, besides two mentions of "night," how the gloom is evoked with "pitchy darkness" and "murk."

I'm not sure I want to know *why* I write. But I don't mind talking about *how* I have written certain of my stories.

How I Wrote Certain of My Books is a title that has always lingered in my mind, not because I have read the book and know it well but because of the word *Certain*, which sounds a little uncomfortable to me in English, at least as it appears in a title, though more natural there in the original French. The book could be considered a counterpart to Steiner's about how he *did not* write certain of his books.

It is the title of a book of essays by Raymond Roussel and also of the book's lead essay. I have looked it up just now, and only now do I see that via Roussel, John Ashbery enters this essay again—because Roussel's book was translated by Ashbery along with two others of Roussel's admirers and fellow writers, Harry Mathews and Kenneth Koch. Ashbery wrote the introduction to the book. I don't have the book here in the house, but Roussel, I now see when I look at *Other Traditions* again, is one of the six writers Ashbery talks about in his Norton lectures.

In exploring *how* I have written certain of my stories, I have advanced as far as understanding that a story begins with something outside coming in and involving emotion, often pleasure. I write something because it occurs to me to write it. It is in some sense found in a field. And the first pleasure is this encounter with something coming in, or wanting to come in. Something that demands, in an impersonal way, to be formed into something else.

It may be an idea of my own that seems to come to me from myself, or it may be material that is actually outside me: a companionable bug, or a slow-moving cow, or the strangeness of the word *organized* when used for a tropical storm, or an emphatic old woman saying something unexpected that I overhear on a train as she stands over me in the aisle. This material presents itself and makes me want to see it be expressed in a form, a formal form, that is just right. I then go forward writing it without thinking too much, guided by a part of my mind not quite under my control. I do not stop to look ahead toward the end of the story. I do not think about what it means unless I look at it much later, from the outside, and then wonder — though I usually do not — what it means.

Part of the pleasure, then, is handling the language, moving the words around. I place the punctuation so that it does just what I want it to do to my meaning. I see the story evolve. I change this and that to make the parts of a story or a sentence better. I hear, silently, in my head, the way it sounds. Then I see what the story looks like when it's done. I see a story exist that did not exist before. It has come into being from the collaboration between the more conscious, controlling action of my mind and the more intuitive, impulsive, and associative action of my mind.

But the pleasure of writing is a demanding one because of the unrelenting demands of the writing – for just the right syntax, the right balance, the right sounds, the right words, the right spellings of our often strange English words. But then the strictness of the demands is part of the pleasure.

Other emotions may come in along with the pleasure of encountering the material. I often relish human behavior, though I am also, often, horrified by it. But I can relish the language, and the handling of language, even when writing about behavior that horrifies me. I almost always revel in the behavior of animals and insects and even minerals and the phenomena of physics.

I am bemused and a little in awe when I see how long a shadow is, cast by the near-horizontal afternoon sunlight, from a single grain of salt on the kitchen counter. In another story, which takes place on the same kitchen counter, I am sympathetic to a little bug that runs away from my sponge, and feel affection as I imagine, or don't imagine but know, that the bug has business elsewhere. He may simply have forgotten it for a moment until my sponge shoved him suddenly, inadvertently, and off he went. The first pleasure comes from amusement at the sight of the hurrying bug, but a further pleasure comes from choosing to write the word *business* in relation to the bug. But because I have respect for bugs and their well-organized lives, I hope the story does not seem condescending.

In another story, I feel less alone when I am visited by a bug, a bug that stays up late to walk down the page of my book when I am also up late, reading.

Nabokov, too, respected the anatomy and behavior of insects enough – and language enough – to object to Eleanor Marx Aveling's translation of a particular moment early in *Madame Bovary* in which she describes a fly as "crawling." No, he says, full of Nabokovian indignation, flies don't crawl, they walk. I never tire of enjoying his concern for accuracy here and elsewhere. But though I know what it means, can I actually define "crawl"? A translator's habit is to look up a word even when she thinks she knows it perfectly well. He is right, of course; a fly does not crawl; only the little feet of the fly would have touched the inner surface of that glass, with its attractive dregs of cider.

I wrote quite a long story that started with a question about how companionable a few ants might be, for me, in the kitchen, as they hauled away, with difficulty, some small crumbs of Parmesan cheese to wherever their hidden home was, down a tiny hole in the tiled counter. The story went on, almost of its own accord, one part naturally inviting the next, to remember friends of mine, since deceased, who, being lonely, I suppose, once fell into the habit, where they used to live, in Germany, during World War II, of putting out food for a housefly who would join them at mealtimes, and then mourned the fly when it died on Christmas Day.

Other things in our world may anger and frustrate me or make me despair. Those emotions rarely come out directly in a story. They simply continue to abide inside me, having matured deep into my bones over time. They may come out indirectly in a story, or not at all, but if I read it later, I can see that they lie somewhere beneath or behind the story, or in its very fabric. How could they not? since they are part of what I am, and the story is coming from me.

I wrote a story called "The Cows." I did not write it with any intention. I did not even write it all at once—it took three years to accumulate. The way it originated was as simple as looking out the window, or standing by the road looking across the road, and observing the cows, who, over the years, started by being three heifers, then grew up, two of them bearing one calf each. After the two calves were adults, they were taken away. I occasionally wrote down what I saw. After three years, I had eighty-some observations. I made a little book of it, with accompanying photos. Only later did I realize that the emotions involved in this story were not only my various forms of pleasure and sometimes amusement or sympathy as I watched the positions and behaviors of the cows and their calves, as well as the demanding pleasure of setting down my observations of them, but also my pain and sorrow over the treatment of most cows in the world. I could see what these particular cows, my neighbor cows, preferred when given the almost complete freedom they had—to go in and out of the open door of their barn, to drink from a bathtub by the fence, to walk to a particular spot in their large field, in winter to stand still in the snow, broadside to the warm sun. Even when they were larger than their mothers, the calves went on nursing now and then, coming over for a few tugs at the teat, and their mothers stood still and waited for them to be done. All I wanted to do, for my own satisfaction in writing down my observations, was to portray exactly the way these cows looked and what they did, black on green or white or tan, in the field. But maybe I was also relishing their freedom to make their choices.

My story "The Cows" is almost purely descriptions of an undramatic reality—loving descriptions. Though my objective portrayals may not appear overtly loving, there is love in the motivation behind them. And sometimes another emotion shows through—quite a strong feeling on my part, not suppressed, determining the choice of what I describe.

My emotion was for the plight of cows, and animals in general, subjected to human manipulation or intrusion or territorial takeover. But did I also love these particular cows? Probably, even though one of them charged me when I got too close to her calf (though there was a fence between us). She did not recognize *with any gratitude* that I was the one who, on a particularly hot day, had filled their dry bathtub with buckets of water carried across the road from my own well after they had been lowing for an hour or more while the three of us stay-at-home older neighbor women — one up the hill, one a couple of hundred yards down the road, and myself in the house opposite — were growing increasingly concerned.

The lowing of the cows was purely their expression of discomfort, but did it then become communication, to us? Does voiced expression involuntarily become communication when someone responds? Or in this case was it already meant as communication?

I don't believe I put down on paper precise descriptions of the cows in order to transport anyone to the place where I stood as I was looking at them. What I was after was more abstract, almost clinical, despite my loving motivation — an exact match between what I saw, what pleased and interested me at that moment, and the words that would describe it so exactly that there could be no other way to describe it. I had no overall plan for these observations, which were entered in a notebook among other material. There was simply the impulse, each time, to write just that one depiction. Then weeks would go by, or maybe just a day or two, or months, before I was moved to write another description or observation. This matters to the outcome, because if I had conceived the plan for eighty-three observations of the cows in the beginning, I might have been tempted to force the observations to come to me—I mean, I would have gone searching for them. And so the set of eighty-three observations was written by accumulation over several years. I simply looked out the window with a natural, recurring, reflexive interest at the field where the cows liked to stand and occasionally walk, very rarely run, and when something I saw struck me, I made a note of it. Was it communication before it was published?

When Karl Ove Knausgaard was asked to write a lecture, which would also be a book, on this same topic of why he wrote, he sat in front of his computer for three days, he tells us in the book that emerged from this, writing nothing. He says it on the first page of the book— "Now I have been sitting here in front of my desk in southern Sweden for three days without making any headway" — and he says it again on page 39, though he has written quite a lot already: "I have been sitting in front of my screen for three days, not knowing what to say — or rather, not knowing how to say it." Then he tells us that he simply began writing and went forward, more or less without looking back, not knowing what might come next, in the same way, he said, that he wrote his multivolume controversial — at least to some members of his family, who found it traitorous — novel *My Struggle*.

If, having been asked why I write, I were to choose to write this essay in the way that Knausgaard wrote his own — he says, anyway, whether truthfully or not — in answer to the same unanswerable question, plunging forward without looking back at the beginning until I was quite a long way in, I might run the risk of discovering, when I came to revisit the beginning, that some of my ideas had changed and that I no longer agreed with them. We change and change again within the space of even just a few months, even physically — a "condition" develops or a condition goes away. But we change our ideas, too, especially if we are reading one book after another and thinking and talking about what we are reading. Or I might find that an idea of mine had not changed but I no longer wanted to keep it in the essay.

When, early this year, back in late winter, I started thinking of ways to begin this essay, and, being tempted to write only about other writers in answer to the question posed to me, was considering both why and how other writers write, I was reading a book I had been given for Christmas called *The Wheelwright's Shop*, by George Sturt.

It was not an obvious choice of a book to give to someone like me who was not particularly interested in woodworking and was not thinking of building a wagon. Farm wagons and their construction was not an interest of mine – though it might be an interest of another reader. I haven't yet asked my friend why he gave it to me.

The book is a very thorough account of the wheelwright shop that Sturt inherited from his father and his grandfather before him. Sturt's ambition was to be a writer, but he was also dedicated to managing the shop and looking after the work and the men who did the work. He had some skill in the elements of building a farm wagon, but relatively little, as he admits. His account goes into extremely technical detail about how each part of a wagon was made at that time – from the 1880s past the turn of the twentieth century. The level of detail is often overwhelming, though the writing of the book is highly deft, pleasing and sympathetic. There is a glossary at the back, but quite a few terms are included in the body of the book that are not explained there.

The friend who gave me *The Wheelwright's Shop* is a sculptor acquainted with the hand-working of made things, with, against the wall of his studio, a set of excellent worn and beautiful old tools inherited from his father, who was for thirty-five years a highly skilled pattern maker in a pump factory. So he himself is a specialized reader, primed to be interested in an account of the finer details of a woodworker's shop. I am not so primed, unless by being generally prone to taking an interest in the way things work, mechanically, and the way things were done in earlier times, and to admiring a good old tool, especially one with the soft patina of a worn wooden handle. As I read along, I could see that some parts of the book would be of interest to a wider readership and some only to a narrower.

But when I talked to my friend about this later, it turned out that his woodworking skill and background, his familiarity with the handling of fine tools, and his admiration for fine craftsmanship were not the only reasons he was interested in this book. He was also interested for sociological reasons – he is reading it now for the third time, feeling it is an extremely important book in the context of the transition from craft-based production to industrial manufacturing.

He also observes that Sturt's meticulous and methodical approach to the writing of the book mirrors the meticulous, methodical process of the skilled woodworker, that Sturt's training in wagon-making is reflected in the way he went about making this book.

If I found Sturt's book tedious at times, why did I go on reading it?

If you are given a book as a present, or someone has recommended it, then you have that impetus to read it as well as companionship, if your friend has already read it. That support may sustain you when you falter. I did continue reading it even though Sturt went into such detail about nothing much more than everything one could say about building a wagon – or a dung cart.

Even my friend admitted that parts of the book, sometimes extensive parts, dragged, even for him.

Besides my interest, small though it was, in the making of a wooden farm wagon or dung cart, there was my curiosity about life in Sturt's village in those times. But beyond what I learned about earlier ways, perhaps I went on reading because of what I learned that was simply new to me, as, for instance, that a blacksmith did not wish to admit sunlight into his shop because the bright light made it difficult for him to perceive and measure the precise intensity of his fire — which he had to know in order to work with it; or that a carter might ask him for a slight modification in a part of the wagon to suit *a special horse* or *a special bit of hilly road*.

In earlier times there was greater silence, of course. At one point, Sturt tells us he could hear a wagon coming toward the shop down the road three miles away. At another point, he says the quiet was "just broken — or emphasized — by tinking from the near smithy or by mallet strokes from the wood shop." Moreover, in earlier times, objects were built to last. A dung cart or a harvest wagon was built to be heavily used for a lifetime. Repairs had to be made now and then, and parts replaced, but the wagon endured.

I experienced, as I read the book, changes in the attractiveness of the text. At times, I had to force myself to read it, I had to push my reading ahead when the subject became too technical for me, more technical, on top of already technical, and I somewhat lost interest. And then, at other times, the effect of the text was quite different, I was lifted by it and carried along, quite effortlessly, as when Sturt began describing one of the more eccentric men in his shop, or how the shop was opened in the morning, the shutters taken off (no windowpanes), or how children and old men and women came to the shop to buy bags of wood chips for fires — a task for the very young and the old. Sometimes pushing my way forward in the reading and sometimes being carried along, I found the reading of this book unusually physical.

Of course, the text even when highly technical could still remain interesting to me, for instance, how different species of standing wood — trees — were chosen for different parts of the wagon, such as elm for the stock (nave or hub); how the wood was seasoned for a surprisingly long time; how, in the yard of the shop, the wood was sawed simultaneously from below, by a man standing in a pit, and from above, by a man standing on level ground, who had the easier job; how very difficult it was to stand down in the pit for so many hours. How the *form* of a nail had to take into account the *wearing down* of the wheel. How the sawdust from dry timber, mostly oak, was useful for curing bacon. How logs were marked with Roman numerals because to cut rounded numbers into the wood would have been so much more difficult. And so on. The degree of detail and necessary refinement in the shaping of the wood was continually surprising – to one who had never built a wagon.

My focus, as I read, was close if Sturt kept it close – for a page or two the focus was on the handles of the tools the workmen used, which they made themselves. Then he would abruptly allow my focus to widen, once back to the time of Chaucer, once out across the English Channel to Alsace.

Sturt describes the way an admired craftsman, George Cook, put the spokes into a wheel, comparing this wheel to one in *The Canterbury Tales* – a twelve-spoke cartwheel. Abruptly he has flown me back in time several hundred years to Chaucer's century, but also, interestingly, he has linked a wheel that really existed in his own shop to Chaucer's fictional wheel, thereby also bridging the gap between reality and fiction and gaining for Chaucer's wheel a different status, closer to that of an existing wheel.

Of George Cook, he says he knew no one like him in any English book at all, but that what Cook called to mind for him was the "village flavor" in the tales of the Alsace in the works of Erckmann-Chatrian. I have not yet investigated the works of Erckmann-Chatrian. I will. If those tales were fictional, then he has done the same work of bridging his own village to a fictional one in Alsace.

But as I thought about it over the months, I began to understand that there was more to it.

Surely my interest was sustained by two other elements that matter to me in a book. One is the author's character as it comes through — in other words, the voice you listen to, the company you keep, for the quite long time it takes to read a book, especially a book with nothing at all, or very little, that you would ordinarily call plot or suspense or even argument — this was not the kind of book in which you want to know "what happened next." What happened next was that the stock was marked for the first augur holes, "preliminary to mortising it for the spokes. A tricky job, this."

The other quality is the style of the writing itself.

My friend may have known I would appreciate the skill and even beauty of Sturt's writing — and how odd it is, when I think of it now, to imagine a beautiful style of writing, particularly a sensitivity to sound and rhythm and balance in phrasing, serving the subject of how to make a farm wagon.

Sturt's tone shifts subtly as he moves from a lighter, more amusing moment to a graver or more matter-of-fact one.

He relieves a more technical account by breaking off to paint a more lyrical scene.

He deals out short, emphatic sentences: "If they didn't, you knew it"; "He felt that it looked right"; "A tricky job, this."

His language is sometimes the language of a time even farther in the past. For instance, he uses the word *benighted* to mean overtaken by night or darkness.

His writing is above all exact. It must be all about exactness, because the correct construction of a wagon is all about exactness; approximation has no place in it. The entire craft of making a good wagon is about exactness, so Sturt's book must give an account of that, which he does mostly without metaphor. The exact handling of a tool, the exact taking of a measurement, how exactly a wagon was designed to fit its environment, how exactly the tines were set in a wooden harrow, the exact modification of a particular wagon's structure to accommodate the width of ruts in a dirt lane that might have been carved over many years. The book is all about the exact skills developed and modified over hundreds of years. Sturt tells us, for instance, that an apprentice would need a good seven years to learn the trade and would continue to learn more after that. My friend tells me that his father arrived at the factory with already considerable woodworking skill, but was then still considered an apprentice pattern maker for the next seven years.

Sturt's care for detail, specificity, and precision in his descriptions of the processes of putting together a wagon animates all his descriptions in the book — it is his way of seeing things: when George Cook moves from his country cottage to a house in the village, says Sturt, he now has, on his walk to work, "three or four minutes of level street."

Sturt is an agreeable companion in my reading — even a moment, just a hint, of wit, intelligence, or good humor as he narrates is enough to signal this to me.

He is also sympathetic because fallible – he is still learning the craft in the shop, and he makes mistakes. He admits his limitations: "Of the stock (the nave or hub) I hardly dare speak, such a fine product it was, and so ignorant about it do I feel."

Even the particular aptness and variety of his word choices reflect well on him. And what is Sturt's relationship to language generally? It is a question that I can't help asking of some other writers, too, as I read them. A writer whose relationship to language is condescending, or arrogant, or careless, disappoints me, no matter how clever or masterful he or she is. Sturt's attitude is as respectful to language itself as to the workings of the shop and to his readers. And he depicts with empathy and admiration the other human characters in his account.

Sturt's affection for the men in the shop shows through in his description of the blacksmith at work: "So hot the expanse of iron was, even Will Hammond could hardly bear his fingers near enough to place the punch. He held his little finger away like a fine lady holding a teacup: he blew on his finger-nails to assuage for a moment the intolerable heat, or he plunged his whole hand into the water-trough at the front edge of his hearth. . . . Black-haired and sweating, he bent over the anvil, while his hammer-hand rose and fell strenuously. I saw how his shirt grew moist, heard his genial laugh as he turned back to his fire again . . . ; but I suppose only the anvil and the hot iron were ever truly in position to see a blacksmith's face when he was hammering his hardest."

Reading *The Wheelwright's Shop* took me some months, and after I was done, it remained in my mind to "bother" me — in the good sense of posing a question. Although the friend who gave me the book had read it, and thought I would like it, and although I had read it, and liked it, in the end, it did sometimes border on the tedious and I had to wonder how many other people would be likely to read it.

If I couldn't imagine many people would want to read it, I had to wonder just why Sturt had taken the trouble to write it and write it so painstakingly and thoughtfully.

But I was starting from a faulty premise — that you write a book only if people will be interested in reading it. That may be the premise of the publishers. Most of them, though not all, don't choose to publish a book if it will have only a few readers. But this premise is not necessarily a writer's. (Not *necessarily.*)

If Sturt didn't expect much of an audience, that evidently did not matter to him. He wrote his book to share with those few who were interested or at least willing to read it with varying interest.

No, I am wrong again—he did not write it *in order to share it,* though I can imagine he wanted to share it and was glad of an audience; and it may indeed have mattered to him whether his audience was large or small.

In this book, Sturt did not court an audience but asked his readers, despite our possible impatience—but again, I'm not sure this occurred to him—to join him in considering a farm wagon and all parts of the wagon and exactly how they are made and fitted together and why.

He shows that he is explicitly aware of his readers and that he wishes to be considerate of their attention, as he asks himself—though of course we are listening—in reference to the hanging of the wheels on an axle, "Shall I tell how the arms were finally fixed in the axle-bed (and how that was fixed to the body) with clips and clip-pins, to say nothing of tail-pins? It isn't interesting enough, perhaps. . . . More interesting is it to note how the axle-bed, ready at last, was lightly shaved-up with the draw-shave wherever possible." In fact, in quoting this passage, I have improperly (because silently) substituted "axle-bed" for his "ex-bed." But you must search the glossary at the back to find this entry: "EXBED. The usual name for axle-bed," "usual" perhaps meaning colloquial — if you can even imagine what an axle-bed is. Even my friend, with his greater background knowledge and priming for this book, and with the glossary for reference, found himself confused on certain pages as he tried to imagine a certain process, despite Sturt's clarity of writing.

But I find myself thinking two contradictory things about his audience of readers. The first thing I think, before I think again, is that Sturt crosses the line between what is interesting enough to write about, for a general reader, and what is not. Then I realize I am starting from the wrong premise again: although perhaps he did want to interest a general reader, or did not want *not* to interest him or her, that was not what determined what he included in this book. So perhaps he did not need to consider it even for a moment.

Why did George Sturt write this book?

Sturt's reasons for writing the book seemed to me, finally, completely pure and basic. He wrote it because he cared enough about the subject and had enough to say about it to write about every aspect of it that he chose to, no matter how few readers would be interested. And he thought this account of exactly what the title says — a wheelwright's shop (and what went on in it) — should be written.

He was in all earnestness dedicated to recording in close detail something that existed in his time and before his time and that had value to him and value in itself. He saw that the art of the wheelwright was disappearing from rural England, and would entirely disappear before long, no longer needed. He wrote it all out because it had been his world for so long, because he valued highly the skill and experience necessary to do it well, and because he wanted us to know it, or, rather, he wanted it to be known. He wanted to record exactly what went into making a wagon, a cart, or a wheelbarrow, what the tools for working it were called, the fine, refined skills that were required to do it, and the many years it took to acquire those skills, because he was one of the few, maybe almost the only one, qualified to write this particular book since he had practice, proficiency, and ambition as a writer and had also acquired some of the skills of the wheelwright and a great deal of knowledge about those skills.

So he did not want to carry that knowledge to the grave with him without imparting it first, whether or not anyone was interested. Once he had recorded it, it would be there to be read, whether or not anyone read it. So it was to record it, memorialize it, and almost certainly also, as he wrote it, to admire it, to relish it in the telling, to remember and relive it, that he wrote his book.

In this exhaustiveness and fixation, Sturt's book resembled another book I had been steadily reading, though with long intermissions as I gathered the will to launch into it again: J. A. Baker's *The Peregrine,* which is really just as narrow in subject matter. The entire book is confined to the flat marshes of the Essex coast of England. In the several chilly months covered by the book, the creatures populating it are mostly the same, with only minor shifts or variations — the certain types of birds of that watery estuarine landscape, especially the raptors — and the only action is the action of the birds, the weather, the landscape, and the author, besides, very rarely, another human in the distance, perhaps a farmer on a tractor. Nothing much happens except what you would expect of the water, the wind, the clouds, the sun rising and setting, and the birds — which fly up into the sky, or out over the water, or down to bathe in a stream, or land in a tree, remain sitting on a branch, groom themselves, doze, sleep, tear apart their prey. And the author walks through their territory or sits watching this or that.

The interest from page to page is partly in the action that Baker narrates to us, but partly, as in the case of Sturt, in the skill and beauty of the way he writes it. Before coming to this book, I had only a little interest in peregrine falcons, and it was soon spent. So for me to continue reading it, this book, like Sturt's, depended greatly not only on the way it was written but also on the character and personality of its author, in whose company I would be spending a considerable amount of time — and my respect for him included marveling at his dedication, which caused him to go out early on a brisk or cold morning, day after day, and stand still or walk slowly for many hours watching the creatures in the sky and on the land and water (whereas I preferred to read the book in a warm house, sitting or lying down, my head up on a pillow, being transported to his landscape in comfort and almost effortlessly).

Baker's was a feat of writing, I decided. How, otherwise, do you manage to narrate with such resourceful variety what is essentially the same thing day after day and page after page? The richness of the writing is an extraordinary thing to study, once you begin looking at it. How many ways can Baker describe the plumage of a tiercel? The flight of a pigeon? The way a raptor tears apart its prey? The appearance of a very small owl? (He found the creature amusing and – giving us insight for a moment into what guided his approach to writing the book – admitted having to fight the impulse to anthropomorphize it.)

Whereas Sturt's exactness requires, and draws on, a wide, specific vocabulary but not much metaphor, Baker's, so strictly factual and confined to one landscape, not only depends on an equally wide specific vocabulary for describing fine shades of differences but also admits into his narrative an entirely other, colorful scene via metaphor, as in this brief description that includes gentle play on the sounds of the words while pairing a simile and a metaphor drawn from another part of the landscape: "Five minutes later he lifted into air again, circling, gliding, diving up to brightness, like a fish cleaving up through warm blue water, far from the falling nets of the starlings."

This book, and Sturt's, too, as one reads them, are calm places. Is that part of their appeal, in our troubled world? There is only the slightest hint of emotion in them — a glimmer of amusement or embarrassment, wistfulness, melancholy in Sturt's, some pride in Baker's, some admiration for the raptors. And, written before our time, they are untouched by our contemporary woes but also don't include current events of their own time, except occasionally and by implication in Sturt's book. (The changing demands of the wagon trade, the introduction of new — factory-made — parts.) Is Ashbery's *Other Traditions* also a place of refuge? I step into this other, calm place with this calm companion discussing things that interest me and interested him and, as I remember, at least, the discussions did not include anything about politics or world events. (I haven't checked for that, though.)

Part of the time I am writing this essay — just now — I am riding in a train south along my own local estuary, the lower reaches of the Hudson River in New York State. The river has its origins miles north as a narrow stream — a trickle? — issuing from several lakes but mainly from Lake Tear of the Clouds in the Adirondack Mountains. I once said something to a friend about the fact that he lived on a river. No, he said, he lived on a creek. It was a wide creek, the Rondout Creek. I thought I knew at least that his creek emptied into a river — that is, the Hudson River. No, he said, at that point in its course it was not a river but an estuary.

An estuary is tidal. Maybe for this reason, the Mahican Indians called the Hudson River Muhheakunnuck — "Great Waters Constantly in Motion."

As I ride south, if I look to my right up into the tall trees with bare branches that line the water here — but the only bare-branched trees are, since it is June, the dead trees — I may see a raptor. Just as I form these words in my head, looking out the window of the train in search of one, I see a bare-branched tree and a bald eagle clutching a branch near the top. Farther down the tree is a second bald eagle — a bonus. Then the eagles are gone from sight, behind me upriver, and I look away, to write this down. In doing so, of course, I miss a piece of the passing landscape and other trees with perhaps other raptors.

Time passes as we write, and life goes on, with its briefer and more extended story lines. There are other things happening in my life right now and, as I continue writing, each story line will reach some sort of resolution and then be past. Problems will arise, and at first I will find them daunting. Then I will begin to solve them and they will seem manageable and they will pass. I will find some events or some things people say upsetting, at least mildly so, and then my upset, too, will diminish and recede into the past—usually. And my moments of pleasure, too, will recede behind me like the landscape seen from the train window.

This spring, as I thought about this essay and made notes for it and wrote parts of it, the following things happened. A much-loved cat died and was buried behind the house, with difficulty, in the mostly frozen earth. I heard that a distant friend whom I hadn't seen for many years was facing her impending death.

She faced it, I was told, with a matter-of-factness that was admired. Another friend, a closer friend, faced his own impending death, also stoically. He was annoyed by the word *brave* when it slipped out of my mouth before I could stop it. I understood his annoyance – it is almost an insult for a living person to call a dying person brave. A third friend was declared, after some suspenseful waiting, to be free of cancer. Then the first friend died. Then the second friend died, sooner than expected, only two weeks, instead of several months, as I had anticipated, after he had startled me when I picked up the phone by saying, in a strong and completely normal, almost practical tone of voice, "I'm calling to let you know that I'm dying."

In trying to answer the question of why he writes, Karl Ove Knausgaard talks about Hamsun's *Hunger* and the reasons it attracted him so much when he was nineteen years old: "It had to do with closeness and presence – Hamsun follows his protagonist so closely that there is no plot, no construction of character, everything centers on him and what he sees, and it is as if Hamsun thereby describes the world as it comes into being, as it emerges for the main character. The world becomes the present, the world becomes the here and now, and this renders a dramatic storyline perfectly unnecessary, for the intensity of the present is such that everything becomes important and interesting."

I, too, read this book when I was young, young like Knausgaard and young like the protagonist, who seems to be named Knut. The book, though a piece of fiction, became all the more real to me years later when a friend and I visited Oslo and made a plan to have dinner in the premises of the real building in which Hamsun located the home of the fictional woman who (improbably) seems attracted to the starving, ragged, penniless Knut and whom he names Ylajali. Making our plan, that afternoon, for the evening to come, we stood in front of the building *in the very spot* where the protagonist had once stood, both with and without Ylajali – though he, the protagonist, *did not exist.* Our plan was then foiled, to my great disappointment, because we were invited out to a professional dinner in a different restaurant and felt we had to attend.

Here is a little symmetry: I read *Hunger,* with its young protagonist, when I was young, and then, when I was myself getting old, I read Hamsun's last book, a memoir, *On Overgrown Paths,* the work of a very old man. I also walked, with my friend, on the very same overgrown path that Hamsun had really walked on, in the town of Grimstad, where he was confined to an old people's home while awaiting his trial for sedition. He, the protagonist of this book, was real, and this path was real. He was nearly blind and nearly completely deaf, like an old dog. He was confined by law to this old people's home but permitted to take walks. He was not permitted to mail letters, but he disobeyed, walking up and over a steep hill on the overgrown path to reach a small mailbox at the end of a dead-end street in another part of town.

As I thought about Sturt's book, why it was written, who would read it, why the author evidently did not mind much if his readership was quite small, I thought of other books whose authors evidently felt compelled to write them, regardless of audience — single-minded accounts that risked tedium for something that mattered to the author, books that came into being only because of their authors' fascination with a certain subject, without regard for audience, books that were also attractive, likable, sympathetic, even engrossing because of the very dedication of their authors and their good writing. In some way, these books embodied one ideal of writing — books that were necessary to their authors, who did not care if the books were necessary to anyone else. Or at least that was how I imagined it — no concession made to what a reader supposedly wanted. But maybe, given our natural love of communicating, our natural need for companionship, it is not possible, as we write, not to care who will value what we've written.

When I was asked to write about why I wrote and when I preferred instead to think about why other people wrote certain of their books, I thought about Sturt's book and Baker's, but also others. I thought of James Agee's *Let Us Now Praise Famous Men,* Melville's *Moby-Dick* and, because Melville was inspired by it, Richard Henry Dana Jr.'s *Two Years Before the Mast,* as well as — eventually coming to mind — the book Knut Hamsun wrote so very late in his life, *On Overgrown Paths.* Much later, I thought of Elizabeth Smart's *By Grand Central Station I Sat Down and Wept.* Agee wrote a description one and a half pages long of a particular oil lamp, Melville gave over an entire short chapter to the subject of oil lamps in general, and other chapters to types of whales, gam and gamming, whiteness, whales depicted in paint, in teeth, and more.

Dana wrote his book for a public that for the most part did not know the life of a working sailor. At the start of his junior year at Harvard, he had contracted a case of measles. It had left his eyes seriously weakened, and he was unable to read without pain. He decided his best remedy would be a life of adventure as an ordinary seaman—with open air, plain food, and hard work—and so he went to sea on a merchant vessel for a little more than two years, from 1834 to 1836, with an interval of a few months working on the California shore. After he returned, with the encouragement of family and friends, he wrote *Two Years Before the Mast* from the diaries and notes he had kept while on board. There had been any number of seagoing adventures already written, but up to now only one, and an indifferent one, claiming to be factual. Dana felt there was newly awakened interest in the situation of ordinary seamen, but very little knowledge about their life coming from "one who has been of them, and can know what their life really is."

Like Sturt, Dana did not avoid highly technical language out of consideration for his reader (nor did he avoid—though he cautioned readers to expect it—"strong and coarse expressions"). That language was inherent to that world, and Dana wrote from within the experience—how could one describe the action of sailors on board a ship without making full use of terms for the parts of the rigging, the handling of the sails, and so on? And yet the unfamiliar technical language is leavened by language familiar to us, as in this passage, which is dense with nautical terms in the middle and then levels out at the end in language quite plain to landlubbers. The captain has been ordering more and more sail added on the ship, which is already going top speed, now heading back toward Boston: "Waiting for a good opportunity, the halyards were manned and the yard hoisted fairly up to the block; but when the mate came to shake the catspaw out of the downhaul, and we began to boom-end the sail, it shook the ship to her centre. The boom bucked up and bent like a whip-stick, and we looked every moment to see something go; but, being of short, tough upland spruce, it bent like whale-bone, and nothing could break it. The carpenter said it was the best stick he had ever seen."

Readers are brought into the action naturally and vividly, through the language of the workings of the ship's governance, through plain, familiar speech, through simile, and through reported dialogue.

Just as Sturt straddled two worlds, that of the writer and that of the artisan and craftsman, Dana straddled the world of the Harvard undergraduate he had been and that of the ordinary seaman he became for a time. Just as the narrator in Dante's *Inferno* — Dante himself — straddles the world of the living and the world of the dead. Dante reports back to us from the Inferno, as Dana reports back from life belowdecks, as Sturt reports back from the workshop.

Both Sturt's book and Dana's were bearing witness, recording in close detail something that existed in their time and had value to them and value in itself, and in the case of Sturt's book, something that was vanishing. In the case of *Two Years Before the Mast,* it was also Dana's explicit intent to record a way of life that he felt more people should be aware of — because he had seen the many hardships an ordinary seaman endured and wished that way of life to be more publicly known, not because it was disappearing – although of course it would eventually disappear, after some years, in a future that Dana did not foresee – but because with more public attention to the welfare of seamen, their hardships might be diminished.

In giving full accounts, all the books I have been thinking about rely on attentive and precise observations of the physical world they are examining. That is true of Melville's novel (for instance, the action of a harpooner); Agee's study (the dense page devoted to cataloguing the smells of the tenant cottages, with their sources and physical qualities); Baker's months-long report on the tiercels (the variety of their feathers, how the birds "stooped" to kill); Sturt's account of the shop; and also Robert Finch's *A Primal Place* (1983), with his detailed notes on the life in and around the kettle-hole bog behind his Cape Cod house, in autumn, in winter – the watery creatures of the bog, the birds in the trees. As he portrays himself, Finch is capable of remaining for an hour at a time bending over the edge of the water. He brings himself into the narrative only as observer, like Baker; what matters to him is the water strider or the polliwog. In his fixedness by the water he is like the unflinching sharp observer Annie Dillard in *Pilgrim at Tinker Creek,* another lover of the water strider! And although Dillard is a more actively present participant in her book, in her and Finch's stillness in the landscape, when they need to be still, they are both like Baker.

When, asked to write about why I wrote, I thought I might write only about how other writers wrote, I thought not only about writers who were willing to risk being tedious but also about writers who were in other ways difficult for some readers but similarly willing to be strange, to write about a certain subject, and in a certain way, *no matter what*—which to me is a sign of an essential dedication. I thought of the fiction of Gertrude Stein; the bleak, withholding poetry of the stridently opinionated Laura Riding; Robert Musil's extended (three-volume), unfinished novel *The Man without Qualities*; Walter Benjamin's unfinished Arcades project (which initially proposed to be a mere newspaper article, was then expanded into an essay, then grew continually over about thirteen years to epic proportions, was evidently on its way to being *interminable,* but remained as it was when Benjamin fled Paris before the advancing German troops and then died in the Pyrenees); the still strange to us poems of Emily Dickinson, with her willful incongruities and native eccentricity; the always surprising fiction of Ali Smith, who has written, for instance, a novel in which one of the two main characters is dead and another novel that was published, and may be bought and read, in two alternative orders; or *The Gray Notebook,* the diary of the Catalan Josep Pla, who took the slim record he had begun on his twenty-first birthday, covering just twenty months of his life, and spent the next fifty years annotating and elaborating it to create the thick book he finally published.

Pla showed me a thing that a writer could do, that I am in fact tempted to do, as Ali Smith has shown me something else possible that I hadn't thought of in prose writing. I already know the familiar forms, and I like to spend time reading those forms, as though embraced in a comfortable armchair — I have most recently read the otherworldly love story *The Outward Room* by Millen Brand, set in 1930s Manhattan, where you would still find a small graveyard on a corner in what is now Midtown; and Agee's *A Death in the Family,* only almost finished, which stays so beautifully entirely within the bounds of a conventional novel—but at other times I want to read something more demanding and difficult.

I still have a shelf on which I've put, over the years, books whose forms interest me, meaning whose forms tempt me, where the Josep Pla diary should be. One of the books still there is another fat one, Han Shaogong's *A Dictionary of Maqiao.* It is a novel whose story unfolds (over nearly four hundred pages) through the definitions of words in a language spoken only in a small village in rural China.

And I have almost forgotten—though it was never on that shelf—Stendhal's most remarkable *Life of Henry Brulard,* his autobiography, told rather dryly but amusingly in the first person and containing hand-drawn diagrams of his memories as described in minute detail.

As I roam around among the books that border on the tedious and enter the territory of the difficult, I ask myself why I have thought of them together. Is it, in some cases, their insistence on inclusiveness?

This insistence: it is true of Melville (a two-page chapter on ambergris); Agee ("I shall not fully list the contents of the bureau drawers" opens a fifteen-line paragraph describing some of those contents, including the colors and patterns of the worn and creased Christmas wrapping paper that is used by the family year after year); and Walter Benjamin, whose book, unfinished as it is, measures two inches thick and weighs just under four pounds on my kitchen scales.

We know that the over-four-hundred-page *Let Us Now Praise Famous Men* originated, in 1936, as something much more limited — an article commissioned by *Fortune* magazine to report on conditions among sharecropping families in the South during the Great Depression. But perhaps Agee, too, became so fascinated and moved by the smallest details of the lives of the sharecroppers that he was drawn into describing the oil lamp in front of which he was sitting one evening, or one family's Sunday-best clothing down to its smallest stain or tear. He admits, in his introduction, to an intention to be "exhaustive." Like Finch and his bog, he sometimes figures in the story himself, as when he expresses his uneasiness (bent over the bureau drawer) at being thus a spy in a humble home, but at other times he prefers to recede wholly into the background. (Whereas Dillard, by her creek, is almost always part, even center, of the story.) Agee's volume, large as it is, was projected by him, by the time it was finished, to be merely the first of three.

As for Melville, his intentions for *Moby-Dick* also changed in mid-stream. He had previously written more conventional or straightforward novels of adventure, and more popular ones — for instance, *Typee* and *Omoo,* which were based on his own adventures at sea. He began *Moby-Dick* with the same sort of novel in mind — another seagoing adventure, this one about a whaling voyage. Although he had written to Dana, a couple of months after beginning the book in early 1850, that he was halfway into it, calling it "a strange sort of book," it abruptly changed direction that summer and began to expand, taking on an eccentric and surprising life of its own. Whereas Melville had originally thought to be done writing it by the end of the summer, he spent another whole year working on it, and as the weeks and months passed it grew into the vastly more ambitious, outsized, even monstrously heterogeneous, thrilling and, to some, puzzling book it became.

The books I was thinking of had something more in common than eccentricity, single-mindedness, a willingness to risk tedium, and a willingness to lose readers, and that was the care and interest of the writing.

This must be one of the things that saves the books from tedium or allows us to forgive it. But doesn't that leave out—or does it? maybe not—the intelligence behind the writing? Can there be really fine writing without high intelligence?

So, there is the passionate commitment to the peculiar subject combined with the close observation, the intelligence of the writing mind, and the high quality of the writing. But perhaps that list leaves out the heart—warmth, compassion, affection. Sturt's heart is very apparent in his affection for the men in his shop and his admiration, even fondness, for the age-old craft. And perhaps Dana's is apparent also, though not as explicit, in his concern for the lives of the men on his ship.

But heart is not always evident. I don't know that heart is evident in Elizabeth Smart's novel. The pleasures of that text come from other sources—maybe from her defiance of norms and from the violent and mystifying beauty of her at times crabbed prose style?

I was also tempted to expand infinitely on the material of one book of mine, and that was my "translation," into easier language, of a children's book called *Bob, Son of Battle* about two rival dogs and their masters in a sheep-herding community of northern England. As I wrote my version of the novel, I found myself researching ever more thoroughly the culture and world of the Cumbrian sheep-herding communities: sheep, sheepdogs, shepherds, the shepherds' sheep-counting systems, shepherds' crooks, the carvers of shepherds' crooks, the Cumbrian landscape, and so on. Each thing I researched led me to something else, my interest never flagging. I researched also the author of the original book, Alfred Ollivant: the lives of his ancestors, his own life, his military academy, and his disabling horseback-riding accident, which affected his health forever after and led to his beginning to write. I looked Ollivant up in census records. I found a newspaper article describing his wedding. I read other articles reporting the guests at seaside hotels, always listed in order of rank and importance. I looked up the probate records for Ollivant's estate after his death. I searched for, and found, his grandchildren. I corresponded with two of them and went to visit one on her dairy farm south of London. I sat down to supper with her and her family and after supper stood in their barn, wearing borrowed Wellington boots and sipping a homemade sloe gin, and watched a calf being born. I listened as her son told me about the individual personalities of his cows, especially how one cow, curious by nature — always walking over to see what was going on — had given birth to a calf that was equally curious.

I did nothing with all of this researched material except compose as many endnotes to the book as I could justify. But if circumstances had been a little different in my life, I might have let this book grow into something much larger.

Most of my stories are not tedious, but not all of them. A story may turn out to be tedious if it needs to be, or at least one of them did, "Letter to the Foundation." This story is narrated by a character who is herself wearisome, very repetitious about some things that are worrying her to do with spending money, and although the problems are interesting in themselves, the long-winded story she tells goes on and on, as she circles back more than once. Let her be wearisome, I thought — that's the way she is.

The other instance I can think of is not a story but my quite long essay about learning Norwegian. To me it is the opposite of tedious. But that is to me — I'm the one who wanted to write it. In this case, willing to be exhaustive like George Sturt and his wagons, I could not leave out the smallest detail about how I learned Norwegian blindly, without any help — which was by opening to the first page and beginning to read a book in Norwegian, with no dictionary, no grammar book, and no teacher! That was my rule, in what felt like a great experiment — no help from outside. The essay as printed would have been even longer if I had not been restrained by the editor. There are still hundreds more words of that essay on the computer and on paper. Because the experience excited and fascinated me so, it was important to me to record it, just as the skill required to make a good wagon, one adjusted even to the width of the ruts of those country roads it was to travel on, mattered to Sturt.

Sometimes, like Sturt, I write to record a particular experience. Or rather, to replicate, to relive, through the writing of it, the experience I had — in the case of learning Norwegian, it being like jumping into a cold, clear, deep body of water, maybe the pool in a disused stone quarry, without knowing how to swim, and yet swimming.

Brigid Brophy called Elizabeth Smart's novel *By Grand Central Station I Sat Down and Wept* "one of the half-dozen masterpieces of poetic prose in the world," but Angela Carter in a review described it as being "like *Madame Bovary* blasted by lightning." (These quotes are printed on the cover of my edition.) Some of that prose remains opaque to me, probably because its logic is so interior to Smart. The connections from one sentence to the next, and sometimes even the meaning of an individual sentence, may not be clear. I can keep rereading and trying to puzzle the sentences out, or I can just read for their surface value without trying to understand. In some passages, the book's strange prose, ever shifting in its diction and tone, is dense with impossible or elusive metaphors, such as "On her mangledness I am spreading my amorous sheets" or "Shame copulates with every September housefly"; in another passage, in exquisite juxtaposition, the questions posed by a border policeman examining the morality of the main character's behavior alternate with quotations from the Song of Solomon heard only in her own head:

> What relation is this man to you? (My beloved is mine and I am his: he feedeth among the lilies.)
>
> How long have you known him? (I am my beloved's and my beloved is mine: he feedeth among the lilies.)
>
> Did you sleep in the same room? (Behold thou art fair, my love, behold thou art fair: thou hast dove's eyes.)
>
> In the same bed? (Behold thou art fair, my beloved, yea pleasant, also our bed is green.)

The subject matter was outrageous at the time, especially to Elizabeth Smart's mother, who makes her own appearances in the book and, outside the book, was so horrified by the story it told—about her daughter's love affair with a married man! her daughter who at first shared this man with his wife! and then took this man for herself! who had children by him! — that she managed to persuade her native Canada — she knew some powerful people — to ban the book's publication there and then acquired all the copies she could and had them burned. Deep in the book, Smart describes this difficult mother as having "eyes . . . like medieval wildmen in her head."

I like to read about earlier times; I'm curious about the ways things were done, possibly better, in the past, in part because I believe those ways, the best of them, could be a resource for managing to survive in the near future, if only people could be persuaded to turn back and adopt them. I have been reading Jonathan Safran Foer's dire book, *We Are the Weather* — dire only because it faces squarely what lies ahead for us. There is one sentence in there — one idea carried in that sentence — that startled me. Or, no, I had had some form of the idea before, so it was not the idea but the way he stated it, and the fact that he stated it, that startled me. It was about eating: "Our ways of eating in the future will have to resemble more our ways of eating in the past." He means, for instance, not only eating locally but also, in agriculture, going back before the era of chemical fertilizers to the older way of nourishing the soil — with cover crops and animal manure, through field rotation, letting fields lie fallow — and that is what some farmers are doing now, with a new consciousness of the importance of the health of the soil, as I learn from many sources, but in a most concentrated and detailed way from a book called *Dirt to Soil*, by Gabe Brown, who is himself a farmer.

Another emotion, sometimes inspiring a story, is delight at certain pieces of language, sometimes language I overhear, such as, in a Starbucks coffee shop, the choice of "drizzle or syrup?" that once mystified an air hostess, in an airport, within my earshot, or the emphatic "Nothing gets better" pronounced by the old woman near me in the train, or a mature woman's modestly offered opinion about Burberry raincoats, once, at the next table in a restaurant.

I am moved by language I hear, which may inspire a story, and by language I read — the clever or subtle manipulation of language performed by another writer.

Why am I so enraptured by a book I am reading these days, James Baldwin's *No Name in the Street*? It may be his company, his voice, and the invitation of his narrative style that cause me to pick up the book again and again, even though I was not intending to read another book of his right now and there are other books I am supposed to be reading. Is it the plainness of his word choices, or their precision, or is it the clarity and balance of his sentences, or the way he uses repetition to take us from one phrase to the next, or his restrained or unrestrained passion? At one point in the book, though in general he uses metaphor sparingly, he was evidently angry enough, during the incident or afterward in the writing, to go to a metaphorical extreme. Here he is portraying a woman whose hostility he has had to confront in a restaurant where he is not welcome. He describes her as having "a face like a rusty hatchet, and eyes like two rusty nails — nails left over from the Crucifixion."

I am arrested by the image. I stop reading forward, and read again what I have just read, and start figuring out how Baldwin manipulated the syntax and word choices to make this image even more powerful: Why does he repeat "nails": "like two rusty nails — nails left over . . . "? Why does he not say the second part all at once: "eyes like two rusty nails left over from the Crucifixion"? I think he repeats "nails" because of the pace he wants for the sentence, so that first we have a chance to absorb on its own the arresting image of two rusty nails before he makes the image even more devastating. Another reason to repeat it may be to convey the sense that he himself stopped at "rusty nails" and then had a further thought, about the Crucifixion.

And why does he say, "left over" from the Crucifixion, rather than just "two rusty nails from the Crucifixion"? There are probably several answers. The words "left over" may make the Crucifixion, and the hammering together of the cross, and the hammering of the man onto the cross, all the more physically real for us. But also, the words "left over" may suggest a thing for which another (thrifty) use could be found, that after the nails were used to crucify Jesus of Nazareth, they could be employed again for other handy, vicious purposes — perhaps every time such hatred as this woman felt was expressed.

I am always reading in the days and weeks while I am writing this essay. If I read Baldwin steadily, a little each day, while I write this essay, as I alternately read his novel and return to writing this, will I pick up some of his fluidity, his skill in creating seamless transitions?

Will I be influenced by his fine distinctions and subtle nuances? Will I read Baldwin, then read a paragraph of my own and revise it upward?

Why does his precision please me so? It is not merely an intellectual satisfaction but almost a physical one: the exact fit of his word to his meaning. His pinpointing of a nuance of difference, too, is physical, like slicing into something. The balancing of his clauses is even more obviously a physical pleasure, just as lack of balance in a sentence, and also a lack of precision, are physically uncomfortable.

There is a book I stopped reading recently because of its imprecision. Carelessness in the choice of a word could betray a writer's imprecise understanding of words but more usually it suggests his lack of dedication or patience or interest. The book I recently abandoned, on the spot, had an interesting structure and device and a good reputation, and I had had it on my shelf for a long time. High time to read it! I thought. But then within pages of the beginning, the writer revealed his carelessness in a brief description of a first sexual encounter by describing a woman's nipples as "fragile."

Nipples are not fragile, they're tough. Even if you have not nursed a baby, you probably know that a nipple can be pulled and pinched and kneaded quite firmly. It may get tender or sore from time to time, but that is not the same as being fragile, which implies breakable. I just recently read the word *fragile,* for instance, used to describe the stalks of two types of plants, blue stars and asters, after they have spent the winter out in the elements and lost considerable substance. Then you do not need a sharp implement to cut them; they are "fragile," and you can break them off close to the crown (wearing heavy gloves).

This author had not chosen his word thoughtfully, to match the real physical quality of a nipple, he had not considered that physical reality carefully, but had reached quickly for a word and gone on writing. I had the impression from other things about the passage, too, that he was writing this description of a first sexual encounter as though within a pair of dashes or parentheses, that he wanted to get on to something else. He was not interested in the scene for its own sake but in using it for another purpose. Nabokov, in his memoir, *Speak, Memory,* would not have rushed through such a scene with a careless choice of words. He dwelt on each part of that book with devoted attention. He was another, like Baldwin, and like Joyce, whose every word was perfectly considered and perfectly suited, and yet whose whole passages move with lyrical grace, as though they had sprung forth most naturally and spontaneously.

I have read such perfunctory descriptions in other writers, too, even writers who are much admired. The writer seems to say to herself, I need to describe a desolate city landscape because my character is driving through it on his way somewhere else, *to a more important scene*. And so the writer quickly puts down the first images that come to mind, useful, appropriate images, but she does not truly enter that landscape for that moment; she does not stop to consider, in a loving manner, the exact qualities of a vacant lot or an old brick tenement that interest her. After all, she seems to say, I just need it for my character to drive through, I don't care about it.

When I encounter something like that carelessness over the quality of a nipple, I lose faith in the writer. Maybe I should have been more tolerant and said to myself, Well, he didn't care much about exact description at that point in the book, but other aspects of the book and later passages may have qualities that I don't want to miss. But reading a book is a considerable commitment of not only time but also thought and even emotion, especially when you have so many books you have brought into the house, when you seem to buy books even compulsively, out of a hunger for yet another book, and haven't yet read most of them, when you have acquired so many that although you have many bookcases, in many rooms, there are still books piled on the floor.

I am reading all the time, and so I am reading all the time that I am in the midst of writing something, and I probably constantly learn more nuances of more things about writing, about ways of writing, or have lessons imprinted more deeply on me, from what I read, especially since I do a lot of analyzing when I read, particularly about what creates the style or tone of a book that pleases me or of a book that I dislike. If a pattern or rhythm pleases me greatly, it is likely to remain imprinted on me somewhere and may come out at some point in something I write. And I may also choose, consciously, to use a form I have encountered in a piece of writing by someone else, as in the books that sit on the shelf with *A Dictionary of Maqiao.*

Once it was the form of David Foster Wallace's "Interviews with Hideous Men" that interested me. I did not like the hideous men or the content of the interviews, but I was interested in the question-and-answer format in which the questions are missing, apart from the letter Q, with only the answers given. I encountered this form when I wanted to write about my recent experience spending a day sitting with many others in a courtroom being willing to serve on a jury and then not being selected, not even being summoned for questioning, but listening to all the questions and answers I could hear across the very spacious room. The interest of the form, for me, being that the reader has to imagine what the questions are.

Having been asked, some months ago, to write about why I write, I needed to choose a form in which to write my answer, if I had an answer, if I could even think of a form. After imagining I could, like Knausgaard, simply start in writing and see what happened, I thought of another possible form, one that I found roomy and comfortable for setting down ruminations and meditations and stories, for hazarding guesses, for including moments of my day-to-day life, and that was a form that had some resemblance to a diary. I had encountered the form now and then over the years, but most recently in *The Art of Translation,* by Kate Briggs, and then, just months before I was faced with this question of why I write, in *Ordinary Notes,* by Christina Sharpe.

Kate Briggs's book moves from considerations of her translation of Roland Barthes to Barthes himself to translation in general to other translators and their books to more personal descriptions her own life and thoughts. Christina Sharpe's book consists of 248 numbered notes and describes incidents in her life, memories, artifacts published and unpublished, and more, always returning to examine from different angles the present phenomenon of Blackness in this country. The form of both books is diary-like in that they are comprised of separate entries, sometimes connected one to the next, sometimes disconnected, and in that both writers speak, on the page, in a personal way about experiences and thoughts and memories and connect this personal narration to the larger and more objective subject of the book. But in each case the book is not written *as* a diary, it is the form of a book written deliberately to have a beginning and an end and an overall shape, unlike an actual diary, while, like a diary, allowing not only for accounts of daily experiences but also for other kinds of storytelling, speculations, and free-ranging extrapolations into philosophy and theory. One reason I like the form is that it offers serious, dense, and concentrated thinking alongside more open personal moments — and the relief of white spaces on the page in which to absorb less familiar thoughts and new ideas — and because it reflects, in a most natural-seeming way, the patterns of our actual thoughts as we interrupt them, return to them, continue them, grow serious, grow tense and then more relaxed, abruptly change the subject, remember small-scale events from our lives and overwhelmingly large-scale events that have occurred out in the world. Trained scholars open their arguments to allow more room for the reader. What we write in this form is an artifice, a construct, deliberately fashioned and formed; it is not (usually) a transcription of our thoughts in just the sequence in which they occurred, but at the same time it is an artificial form that seems natural and comfortable.

I encountered it many years ago in Hamsun's *On Overgrown Paths,* which appears to have been written chronologically, unlike the books by Briggs and Sharpe, which may or may not have been written chronologically. And Hamsun's book has a story line of sorts that depends on chronology and that unfolds through the real time of events in his life, this chronology being regularly interrupted by postponement—postponement of his trial date, postponement of his verdict.

Actually, it is not true that I *thought of* adopting this form *before* writing in this form. I simply began writing in this form, which came naturally to me, in part because of the notes that I took starting early this year, but more probably because it is my habit in any case to take notes constantly on anything that interests me. In part also, perhaps, because I had absorbed the examples of Briggs and Sharpe. I then thought I could *allow* this to be the form in which I would talk about one thing and another to do with why and how I write and why and how other writers write.

It is the beauty of each new day, or could be, that you can start over again—the morning is fresh.

These ever-renewed days determine the form of Hamsun's *On Overgrown Paths*—he says what he can and wishes to say on a given day, stops abruptly usually, and begins anew on the next or another day. The book is thus fragmented by the changing and renewing days, because although in life a new day sometimes continues events and preoccupations of the previous day, often there is, instead or along with these, a fresh event beginning, or a fresh preoccupation. The plot, or story line, does not develop evenly forward, but takes jagged turns.

When you have as your subject the daily events of a very confined and limited life, you write about the most pressing things of a given day, though they may be trivial. Hamsun writes about walking because he is walking each day, and about having no adequate shoes because he needs them to walk. And then about his galoshes, which are broken and which he ties up with string.

He starts with the immediate and the concrete, and sometimes then moves on to the speculative or the philosophical or tells a story from the past.

While he is out walking on his own, he stops to make notes, to write things down, though his eyes are not very good. He calls what he writes "scribbles."

He sometimes recounts interactions with people. He is a famous writer, and sometimes he, the famous writer, is recognized by strangers, but he is also in disgrace at the moment, under house arrest. So, while he is admired by some strangers, others turn away from him.

When I leave Hamsun's book and go back out into the world, I find I have identified so fully with him that I feel, as he sometimes does, that my community is regarding me with disapproval and rejection. In some cases, we give ourselves so completely over to a book, forgetting everything else for a time, that we forget, at least to some extent, who we are. Some in my community here in rural New York State may have mixed feelings about me, but they at least do not look down on me as a Nazi sympathizer.

One source calls Hamsun's book a "novel." I am surprised. I'm sure it was not written as a novel. But I think of this when I come to a long quotation in the book from an "almanac" given to Hamsun by a wandering preacher. The quotation tells a full story. Did Hamsun reconstruct this later, so that it is not, verbatim, true? At another point, he finds a scrap of newspaper in a dump and copies down the dialogue from the scrap, a quarrel between a man and his wife.

This was his last book.

Part of Hamsun's dialogue with the wandering preacher, who carried his shoes over his shoulder, was this:

> "I am going to the city," said the preacher.
> "Then put on your shoes," said Hamsun.
> "I'll wait until I get to where there are people."

In the old people's home where Hamsun is confined, an old man brings in a tobacco plant. From this plant, he plucks dried leaves and smokes them.

From home, Hamsun receives some better shoes. That is all he needs, he says.

On Overgrown Paths is unevenly composed, of disparate elements, over irregular intervals. Weeks or months go by sometimes, while he remains in more or less the same situation.

He is the center. Whatever is of concern to him, he writes about, whether it is how he will repair his galoshes, or life in the psychiatric center, where he was confined for four unhappy months, or his shoelaces, which are too long, or how he sees, on one of his walks from the old people's home, that a neighbor is building a new roof on his house at an angle right up through an older roof, which Hamsun finds peculiar and surely a mistake.

He writes this because it is of concern to himself but also because – I speculate – he must have the confidence born of a lifetime of writing, the belief that what he writes will be of interest to others. Or perhaps he does not consider that question, having by now completely internalized that confidence, so that he writes whatever he pleases, whether or not he has any intention of showing it.

He writes, "One, two, three, four – thus I sit and make notes and write down little odds and ends for myself. Nothing will come of it, it is only habit. Cautious words dribble out of me. I am a faucet that goes on dripping, one, two, three, four – "

He has a little interaction with a neighbor. Hamsun thinks a small spruce tree on the neighbor's property should be saved from being crowded out by a larger poplar. The neighbor smiles but says nothing. Yet, within a few days, the poplar and other nearby large trees are felled, and the little spruce is given more light and air.

Before that, Hamsun, an old man, deaf, with his eyesight failing, would go out in the early evening cutting leaves and branches from the poplar tree away from the proximity of the little spruce. How demented he would have looked, this feeble old man, in the twilight. And yet there were clear reasons for what he was doing.

A parallel story occurred in my own life. Outside a dentist's office, towering above a row of parking spaces, there was a line of majestic white pines. The largest, at the end, truly enormous in girth and height, was being strangled by a vine, also well grown, that reached to the top of the tree and extended out some of its branches. I learned from a receptionist inside the building that the row of pines belonged not to the dentist's practice but to the property next door. I went up the driveway next door and knocked and rang, but there was no answer. I wanted to tell them they risked losing an exceptionally grand tree and that the solution was simple, as I had recently found out from my reading about invasive plant species. There was no need to take down the vine. All one had to do was cut the vine at its base — the rest would take care of itself. At home, I tried to find a phone number for this residence, but eventually I gave up. But if, like Hamsun, I had simply started hacking away at the base of the vine, I would have looked as demented as he, though my reasons would have been sound.

Hamsun writes often in short paragraphs whatever occurs to him, though sometimes he writes longer ones when he gets started on a story. The lengths of the paragraphs reflect very naturally the fits and starts of his mental activity.

His thoughts, and his paragraphs, circle back on themselves — about the little spruce or about his sheath knife, which at first he does not recognize as his.

He circles back to the question of new versus old galoshes. Why would this be of interest to his readers? It is of close interest to him. And he does not dwell on it long enough to exhaust us. Is it that we can tolerate it because we too have our own close interest in the trivial, practical, but sometimes vital things of our own daily lives? Whether I have enough coffee already made for a second cup? Whether to fold the outdoor umbrellas before the rainstorm comes? (The sky is darkening even now.)

Maybe, in fact, there is comfort in asking the reader to share his preoccupations.

He wrote this, about his galoshes, sometime in 1946, not long before I was born. Perhaps I, his future reader, was already in my mother's womb, developing at a quick rate every day. If so, surely my brain cells were already rapidly multiplying, cells in the same brain that would many years later comprehend and appreciate what Hamsun was just then "scribbling," as he says, perhaps sitting on a rock. My mother was instructed to stay in bed for most of her pregnancy because she had had three miscarriages before conceiving me. She was in bed and I, in safety, was growing.

As soon as I had ears, working ears, I was already hearing the sounds of conversation through the watery wall of the amniotic fluid. I assume my brain, from then on, was being conditioned to understand the English language.

Then, when I came out of my mother into the thin air of the outer world, I heard, more clearly and sharply, constant articulate English conversation around me for most of the day, from mother, father, fourteen-year-old sister, six-year-old brother, and a few others (as well as the particular rising and falling woody timbre of my sister's clarinet up and down scales and arpeggios and then off into a melody). It occurs to me only now how the youngest child is born into a much noisier family than the firstborn.

Hamsun died when I was about five years old. Then he was past worrying about the galoshes.

Now, it is close to eighty years since he wrote these entries. On the page, he is actively worrying, and as I read, I follow his argument with some interest, his concern remains very immediate, even though the man is dead and for him the concern is long past. The concern is not really urgent for anyone, neither for him any longer nor for me, it remains urgent only on the page. The page is alive, whereas the man is dead and strangers are the only ones witnessing his concern. As for the galoshes themselves, their remains are somewhere, at least in small or tiny particles, becoming tinier over time or, even if incinerated, incinerated particles.

There is a further episode involving rain gear many pages on, when he is walking in Oslo in inclement weather and a friendly but ultimately troublesome stranger accosts him and tries to get him to buy some more protective footwear—"out in this weather!"

I was conceived about a month after Hamsun's newly scheduled trial date in September '46. Then his trial date was postponed again to "sometime in the summer" of '47, which is when I was born. My birthday is in a few days from right now, as I write this in the very hot July of 2024. Then, a year later, his verdict was at last pronounced in the summer of 1948.

Hamsun makes a passing reference, contained compactly within a metaphor, to a writer named Boganis writing about a dog, a ditch, and a scent. He does not explain the reference to Boganis, either assuming that "we" know it or, more likely, not caring if we don't. I probably didn't look it up eight years ago when I first read this book. I do now.

Boganis, it turns out, was the pen name of the Danish writer Wilhelm Dinesen, who, it turns out, was the father of the now much better known Isak Dinesen, or Karen Blixen. But as a young man in 1873, before he settled into the marriage that produced her, he went off to America and lived with the Chippewa Indians for over a year, hunting with them and becoming integrated enough into the tribe to father a child. Boganis was the name the Chippewa gave him. He wrote a book about his experience. Because I look him up, Boganis and his story, his life, his writing, all of this unfolds for me from Hamsun's metaphor like a paper flower in water.

Hamsun writes, toward the end of the book, that in a hundred years, all of this—what he did during the war, his trial, the verdict—will be forgotten. I would guess that already now, after nearly eighty years, it is forgotten by most people, as the older generations who did care have died and the younger ones hardly know what a Nazi was. And I'm sure he is right that in 2048, one hundred years after, given all that the people of this imperiled earth will have to contend with just to survive, surely almost no one will give a thought to Knut Hamsun—maybe no one will ever think of him again.

I read somewhere — where? — that at the very end of the human era, our entire civilization — all of it, towering monuments and historic ruins — will be compressed down to the thickness, on the surface of the earth, of a piece of cigarette paper.

The trial is over, though the verdict has not been given, and Hamsun is taking his daily walks again, this time from home. He walks for about two hours each day. He says it is no fun, but neither is anything else any fun. Then he says flatly that he should have been dead a long time ago. I find this sequence of statements, though it is gloomy, also unexpectedly comical, as if it is that simple — one, two, three. If this is no fun, and nothing else is any fun either, we should simply die.

Today there is the constant clatter of a backhoe or steam shovel coming from the hillside across the road and down a bit, where they are doing something to the dirt around the new house they have been putting up. It is a hot day. Another noise is the hum of a fan in this room. The little cat is asleep, stretched out on her side, pressed up against me. A dog, not my dog, is asleep outdoors, stretched out on his side in the shade.

Since I am being asked why, in general, I write, I can ask specifically what, exactly, was the purpose of writing that last paragraph, including the backhoe and the small cat?

Maybe I wanted to write that because I wanted to evoke this moment of this day — clatter of backhoe, hum of fan, cat lying here, dog lying outside — so that I could make it permanent. Maybe I wanted to take that reality I perceived with my senses and filter it through my brain and onto the page and let it stick there. I thought of saying that I wrote it so that I could remember this moment later when I read it, but that is not true, since I don't think in such pragmatic terms about writing, unless I am writing in a diary specifically to remember what happened that day.

Also plausible might be that I write it so that I can present this picture or moment to someone else, share my immediate present, not be alone in my immediate present. But I think that's not exactly it either. It is really so that I can have the pleasure of writing parallel sentences about parallel animals, describing on the page in parallel terms how I see two animals in parallel postures — indoors, outdoors — because this can be seen on the page whereas it can't be seen in reality, since one can't see both animals at once, lying prostrate in the heat, both appearing to be tired, even exhausted, unable to move, though we know from experience that they are not, they could spring to their feet immediately and run off, full of energy, if they chose to.

I want to write this, and have written this, but whether I will include it in the essay I don't know. It is one thing to want to write something, and go ahead and write it, and it is sometimes another thing to want to show it, and in what form.

Close to the end of his book, something Hamsun has written about "the present" happens to remind him of his time in America, when he was quite a young man, and he then enters the story of that time and narrates it without a break — for eighteen pages! Then he stops abruptly, steps back from the detailed narrative, and in plain, factual, clear language summarizes the rest in a single sentence: "I went to Dalrymple's farm in Red River Valley and stayed there until after the harvest." The specifics matter to him, though they might as well be arbitrary for us. We don't know Dalrymple's farm—so it is as though Hamsun has become lost in his memories and is speaking now only to himself.

There is a break on the page, and then he returns to the "present" of the writing: "It is three years today since I was arrested. And here I sit."

I'm thinking just now: If you lie still, especially with your eyes closed, and just listen, then you may have the sense that while you are keeping so still, the world continues to move through the course of its day around you, regardless of you. Outdoors, behind the back of my head with my closed eyes, and beyond a line of shrubs and a wooden fence, is the road. Along the road, vehicles pass now and then, not very often, although as each new house is constructed up the road, in the woods east of where I live, there will be another one or two cars going by. Just now, the passing vehicle is the large, noisy truck that picks up our trash. There is the rumble of the engine coming along the road, then the sound of the engine idling, then some odd metallic thumps and thuds preceding the clatter of glass bottles and jars and tin cans tumbling into the back of the truck. Then there is a sound like a rising wind as the truck moves on. You know from this that it is a Tuesday.

When a specific date is given in a piece of fiction or a news report, when the narrative moves from general time to specific time, you know something is about to happen: "As the summer passed, Emily grew more and more bored. But early on the morning of August 2 . . . " And your level of interest and attention goes up. But in this case, when I say it is Tuesday, you know only that the trash was collected, which is not interesting, unless there was something interesting in the trash.

I have the fan pointed so that it blows directly on me now — it is such a hot July day, a hot Tuesday in July. But even though I am trying my best to stay cool, I don't mind that the little cat's warm body presses up against me. She won't sleep with me at night in the bedroom anymore, ever since friends visited for three days with their little dog, which roamed through the house at night, frightening her. But she will lie beside me during the day in the safety of this room.

I am almost finished reading *On Overgrown Paths*. Hamsun is again returning to one of his very minute, unimportant—though to him pressing—preoccupations, this one concerning his cane. But I am as always captivated by the immediacy of his writing: he and the cane "both" habitually fall, and fall away from each other, like two living creatures. I see vividly the angles of the cane and him, in the snow, an old man and his companion, the cane, lying in the snow.

After the bit about the cane, he is almost done, but not quite. He digresses yet again, in the very last two pages, to a story about an old woman with "walking-sight"—which is, he explains, enough sight to walk by. He gives her full name. This old woman appears to have been "high-born," he says, born into a good family, that is the impression she gives to the neighbors watching her. And yet she walks from farm to farm with one errand only: to beg for chewing tobacco for her toothache.

After he tells this surprising story, which seems to flit onto the page and away again as though alighting for a moment from his ample store of memories and concluding with the general statement, "It is good to have walking-sight for years and years," there is a break on the page, and he ends the book with a scanty two sentences:

St. John's day, 1948.
Today the Supreme Court has given its
verdict, and I end my writing.

(After all this time during which we have accompa-
nied him as he awaited his trial and bided his time and
walked, after all this time during which we walked
with him, he does not tell us what the verdict was. It is,
again, as though here he is talking to himself, or writing
for himself. He does not need to announce the verdict,
because he knows what it was.)

I once wrote a story called "Jane and the Cane." I wrote it
before I read Knut Hamsun's description of falling in the
snow with his companion the cane. But perhaps, anyway, I did not need to have read that description to sense
that a cane becomes like a friend to anyone who relies on
it to stay upright and balanced. It is also an odd object
in itself, like a bird or a question mark or an undressed,
spokeless umbrella. Or a person. It may lean against the
wall in a corner of the room, waiting to be useful.

My story "Jane and the Cane" was based on a true
story, as many of mine are, though this one, like most or

even all the others, was a selection from the true story, a shortened form of the true story, and otherwise changed from the lived reality it was based on. I have said that stories "occur" to me, and that there is emotion at the heart of them. This one must have started with a couple of things that pressed on me enough for the story to ask to be told. There was the rhyme in Jane (her real name) and cane. Also the reverberation that the very name Jane set up from so many decades before, back in my childhood, with my love of learning to read in the Dick and Jane books when I was six or so, books that used beautiful, simple, readable words like Jane and cane, though they would not have used "cane." Then there was the absurdity, which amused me at the time, of the two old women, like Punch and Judy, confusing their canes and tiresomely borrowing and returning canes, and complaining, though not hitting each other over the head with them as Punch and Judy might have. There was the absurdity and my amusement, but also their real emotion, which wasn't funny. Then my problem, as it often is for me and for writers generally, was the ending: how to end a story like that, which goes around and around in circles and is absurd? Maybe we become tired of the whole thing, so that's a way to end it. Let the one old woman also be tired of Jane and her cane, and that's the end of it.

But beneath that simple rhythmical, rhyming story, as it came out, there is more — as always, no doubt, some real emotion or emotions of several kinds. There is the sadness of these two women having to fuss endlessly now over canes, after having led a long and more interesting life, when they were both young, and pretty, and witty, and went out dancing; and there is my positive joy in the language as I write it, the sheer joy for me of using rhythmic prose and rhyming words; and, back to the old women, there is also the solace for them of having a close friendship in the neighborhood, even if you annoy each other concerning your canes.

Hamsun portrayed himself, a thin old man, and his cane in the snow, as though both these two linear figures were canes. In fact, he does personify his cane, I now see, when I go back to his description. Is my enjoyment of his image the same as relishing a story of my own, as Ashbery was made ecstatic by reading a poem of his own? No, not quite. But I see now that I have altered Hamsun's image to be what I preferred to remember it as; when I now reread Hamsun's description, it is not the same as the image I saw and remembered – he and the cane, in my memory, explicitly described as being *at angles* from each other in the snow, two linear figures. The angles are not there on the page, I added that image, from what he said. He said:

> Was the cane any support to me? No. We had become companions, but nothing more. When we fell, we always lay far apart from each other in the snow.
>
> As might be expected of companions.

(I don't understand what he means by "As might be expected of companions.")

I am not surprised that I have altered his image. I have done that with whole books. I read the book. It impresses me. It changes me. But then I mis-remember it, turning it into what I prefer it to be. And I have done this to stories.

I have done this to stories. For instance, I altered a short story by Raymond Carver that had made a permanent impression on me (in its altered form) because of a universal truth it embodied. I even altered the title, which I called, to myself, "The Birthday Cake." The bare bones of the story are this: parents order a specially decorated birthday cake for their child, let's say a little girl—boy or girl I can't remember. But on the day they are supposed to pick up the cake, the child is in a serious car accident and is taken by ambulance to a hospital, where she is fighting for her life. Naturally, the parents forget all about the cake. But the baker does not—the cake is ready, and he can't sell it to anyone else. He calls the parents on their home phone, and calls again many times as the days go by, increasingly angry, even menacing. The parents, when they take turns going home to rest between their vigils by their daughter's side in the hospital, hear his messages but are too distraught to respond. That is how I remember it.

This was the good and effective part of the story—the so-called "setup" or "basic idea." When at last I picked up the story again and reread it, after living with my own version for so long, I was disappointed almost throughout. I disliked the title, "A Small, Good Thing." I disliked the handling of the baker's interventions, as his messages became ultimately evil—Carver took it too far, into the territory of the grotesque, instead of keeping it ordinary and human. I disliked the ending, a reconciliation, as the parents at last visit the bakery after the death of the child and the baker offers them his sympathy. I found it not only unnecessary but false — it did not ring true. I had erased all of this from my memory of the story and derived from it what I wanted to derive — the idea that in our parallel lives we each have preoccupations that are central and completely absorbing to us and often entirely irrelevant to another person.

That idea was vividly and dramatically illustrated by something I later found in Flaubert's *Madame Bovary* — reading it so slowly several times as I was translating it — especially in one scene contrasting the grief of a young boy, who has gone off by himself to weep over Emma's death, and another character's suspicion — his certainty, in fact — that the boy has been stealing his potatoes! After seeing what Flaubert was doing with point of view, having been prepared long before, perhaps, by the same theme in the version of the Carver story that I remembered, I wrote a story of my own about this idea after witnessing something local to me here where I live.

Every September, at the beginning of fox-hunting season, there takes place the old-fashioned, traditional "Blessing of the Hounds." There is still fox hunting of a sort near here, though not involving, I'm sure, a real fox. Its routes have changed since the Massachusetts Turnpike was cut through and laid down right across its preferred terrain. Just south of the highway is a hamlet called Old Chatham, and every September, this ritual with its participants and onlookers fills the small, irregularly angled crossroads there. The scene in my story involved not just humans and their preoccupations but also animals and their separate preoccupations, which took very little account of the humans present and their preoccupations—because this characteristic is shared by animals, too. Each insect I see is intent on its own business and does not usually care about mine, unless my actions impinge on its own. My own preoccupation may be to rinse a rag under the outdoor water spigot at the side of the house, and I am completely intent on that. The very small spider hurrying across the pale blue plastered wall next to me is completely intent on getting away from the sudden spurt of water.

Here is my story:

At the Blessing of the Hounds, on the opening day of fox-hunting season, a Saturday (large horses sleekly groomed, men and women in red riding costumes seated on them or holding them by the bridle, a little girl less interested in the horses than in her friend across the road, as small as she is, almost small enough to walk right under the bellies of these tall horses, the duck or goose that can be heard in the occasional silence squawking in the brook down below the country store, the car that now and then approaches this congested small country square and then turns around as best it can, the two pug dogs held on a leash by an elderly woman who says that she has brought them to see the Blessing of the Hounds, the onlookers holding their coffee cups steaming in the cool early-morning air, the pack of hunting dogs milling about loose in the road, tightly controlled by the handler with her long whip, the speech of the Master of the Hounds and the silences as he pauses with bowed head between remarks, when the duck or goose can be hear squawking), I am reminded, at last, of Flaubert's lesson concerning the singular point of view, not by the little girl interested mainly in her friend, the other little girl, or by the duck or goose interested only in whatever it is that is making it squawk, down below in the brook, but by the two pug dogs, as they strain at their leashes to reach one particular spot on the ground, intent not on the horses, the riders, the speech of the Master of the Hounds, the hunting dogs, or the squawking duck or goose, but only on the yellowish-white dollops of foam that have dropped from the mouth of a high-spirited horse nearby onto the dark pavement and that are so strange to them and so fragrant.

St. John's day, 1948.
Today the Supreme Court has given its verdict, and I end my writing.

Despite the fragmented nature of *On Overgrown Paths* and Hamsun's digressive tales, his reminiscences and comments, irregularly longer or briefer, some of which may seem arbitrary, the book he has written, his last book, has a coherent structure in part, or mostly, because of the interrupted but recurring chronological progression of the account of his often-postponed trial and his worry over it. He is waiting, in real time, throughout the writing of the book, and we, as we read, are waiting with him. He bides the time with accounts of his daily life and episodes in his life, present and past, and bides our time, too, with his stories and comments, as we accompany him, once we have chosen to read his book. He is waiting in his own real time, and we are waiting in the vastly shorter period of reading his book, although, in a sense, we are waiting in his real time, too. Then, with the court's decision, the wait is over, the resolution has been reached, so the book can end, and does simply end, abruptly but naturally.

He was approaching ninety years old as he wrote this last book, and he died a few years later, at age ninety-three.

I was just thinking about endings the other day when I received a recently published book of short stories called *Canoes,* by Maylis de Kerangal, translated from the French by Jessica Moore. I skimmed through the first story, about two friends meeting for a drink after a long time of not having seen each other. (The voice of one has changed, disturbingly for the narrator, a continuing motif throughout the story but not part of my point.) The ending of the story is well devised. The two women are sitting outside on a terrace. After describing how the evening had quieted down around them, the narrator says, "The moment had come for us to sing together, and we ordered two more White Russians." Those are the last words. The evening is winding down, but we leave them as they are about to continue *their* evening a little longer, celebrating a tradition of their own. One way to make a good ending, I think, as I read this one, is to imply, or declare, that the story continues *without* us after we have left it. In other words, the illusion we have accepted while reading the story is strengthened because the events that unfold in the story seem to have a continuing life of their own.

When I used to teach writing, I would say to the students that the way to learn something like how to end a story well was by reading many endings they admired, of stories they admired, and figuring out for themselves why the endings were so good. Although the students were sitting in front of me in rows and looking at me, I did not know if what I said was helpful to them or if they even heard it.

The evening quieting down around the characters in that story by Kerangal — "Around us, the terrasse was thinning out" — reminds me of the late hour in Hemingway's "A Quiet, Well-Lighted Place," which begins, "It was very late and everyone had left the cafe except an old man who sat in the shadow the leaves of the tree made against the electric light." It made me think of the older waiter who understands the value of there being a clean, well-lighted café in which a lonely person can come to sit and have a drink. He would have been willing to let the old man have yet one more brandy, though the old man was drunk and it was past two in the morning, whereas the young waiter was in a hurry to go home and refused to serve the old man, more or less driving him out.

The two waiters and their differences of characters remind me, in turn, of the two off-duty bus drivers — one older and compassionate, and one younger and rougher, with his rude comments, for instance, about a young woman he was watching out the window as she waited in line to board—who sat behind me once on a bus trip down to the city, and whose conversation, after it caught my attention and I began listening, I copied into a notebook for almost the entire trip. I used to tell my students, when I taught writing, that you can learn to write good dialogue by studying real speech patterns, by copying down real conversations. And of course character is often nakedly revealed by what people say, especially when they are unaware that anyone is listening.

Today, months after I was asked to write about why I write and thus reluctantly faced a question the answer to which I probably preferred not to know, a partial answer at least to how I write may have come to me by chance in an unusually long email from a friend, a woman who sometimes kindly leaves her own obsessive project of planting on her property more and more native trees and shrubs in what seems to an outsider an already thick and entangled forest to come work with me in the village park where I have embarked on my own obsessive project of planting more and more native trees, shrubs, perennials, and grasses. In her email, after talking about how we might deal with the invasive knotweed that grows on the banks of the creek that runs alongside the park, she made a good guess at how I write some of my stories. She said: "Some of your stories are thought journeys that probably occurred in seconds in your brain but which you then had to stop and write down, possibly adding additional thoughts as you went . . ." She is almost right, except that I don't always stop and write them down, but usually write them down later, at a quiet time. But she is right that I would certainly add more thoughts as they occurred to me while I'm writing down the first thoughts I had, if they seemed to belong in the story.

We may have an idea of where to start, sometimes even how to end, even how long the story or poem will be, but what happens during the writing may be quite unpredictable. Proust is famous for adding more material as he revised *In Search of Lost Time*. It was his housekeeper who suggested that he make accordions of pages taped together hanging off the original pages to accommodate the interpolation of his added thoughts.

My friend went on to say, ". . . all of which takes focus and discipline and time." It's true about focus. I can't write with music on, or if there is an interesting conversation within earshot. The door to my study being opened by someone may be fatal to the words that were just then being dictated by some mysterious other part of my brain and that may scatter irretrievably.

Discipline is not a problem once I begin working. Discipline is more of a problem when I am trying to persuade myself to begin work. There is something out of proportion, or different in kind, about writing, some-thing that does not relate or connect very well to the activities of the rest of one's day. Writing is often hard to go to – but then just as hard to come way from. Once I stop work, the rest of life seems – as it did not before I started to work – relatively uninteresting. Though not always.

My friend is also right that a lightning-quick thought takes time and care to note down, omitting nothing. But time, too, collapses once you are focusing closely and writing at speed. Time passes quickly and painlessly.

Where the village park is, four minutes by car from where I live, in the next hamlet to the north, there was once a working blacksmith within the living memory of one person, my acquaintance Hank, who is old, but not too old to ride a bicycle, though slowly, as slowly as you can ride without falling over, and who comes wavering along on his bicycle, carefully helmeted and goggled, to see what I am planting in the park today. He tells me that when he was young, the blacksmith was still working at the smithy up the road from where we stand talking, and that as soon as he, Hank, as a boy, would come to the crossroads, the crossroads near where we now stand, he would hear the clanging of the black-smith's hammer. The hamlet would have been quieter then, some seventy years ago.

The hamlet, before Hank's time, was a center of industry — upstream from the park was a tannery, the blacksmith shop, a gristmill, a chair factory, and here, at the crossroads by the park, was a general store, and down the road the other way was a church and a lit-tle schoolhouse — but all that commerce is gone now. There is only a bakery, housed in a former tavern, at the crossroads. Down the road, downstream from the park, the ruins of the schoolhouse are barely visible, as they subside further and further into the weeds each year, in a grove of scrubby evergreens backing on the creek. There is no trace of the church.

The Sturt book, during all the months I read it, kept the vivid image of a working blacksmith in my mind.

Ashbery told the interviewer, apropos of titles, what a certain title of a book by the so opinionated and eccentric poet Laura Riding — one of those six poets he wrote about in *Other Traditions* — meant to him. Her title was *Twenty Poems Less*. To Ashbery, that meant twenty poems that she no longer had to write, twenty poems that she had gotten rid of. He went on to say, "That's the way I feel having written a new book. Twenty poems I don't have to worry about."

Russell Edson's problem in "New Prose about an Old Poem" was that he could not get rid of that poem that was not good enough to send out.

This "getting rid of" is the outcome of what begins as "something bothering you" that you have to "do something about." The thing occurs to you; the thing bothers you (pleasurably, though a little anxiously); you find a form for it that fits it perfectly — or rather, the material itself evolves into the form that suits it; you worry it, going through it again and again until nothing about it seems wrong; now you have done something about the thing that bothered you, and in doing that, you have gotten rid of it.

Nabokov said something similar: "Teachers of literature are apt to think up such problems as 'What is the author's purpose?' or, still worse, 'What is the guy trying to say?' Now, I happen to be the kind of author who in starting to work on a book has no other purpose than to get rid of that book."

The little cat has now returned to sleeping with me at night, which is a relief.

This is not something that matters to anyone but me. It may be a fair example of a minor concern that can be allowed—maybe—into a form of writing that includes diary-like entries, such as Hamsun's *Paths*. But maybe Hamsun's galoshes are more interesting than my little cat.

There has been yet another death in the family this month, the month of August, just within the last week.

I have at least two stories about death in the latest book. Since stories are almost always born from things happening in my life, then, if a death has occurred, I will sometimes write about death. One story is called "When We Are Dead and Gone." It is an example of material for a story coming to me not only generally from outside but in this case from immediately outside the room where I was standing.

WHEN WE ARE DEAD AND GONE

When we are dead and gone,
it might be comforting
to hear the quick knock on the door
and the voice from the far side saying,
"Hóusekéeping!"
though we won't be able to open the door.

As may be completely clear from the little story itself, I was in a hotel room when there came that knock on my room door. I don't think the housekeeper came in, or I would have forgotten the idea of writing this story. So I must have thanked her through the door and the door remained closed. But at the moment when she called out in that way, her voice disembodied, sounding from beyond the closed door, which I didn't open, the idea of death and this story came into my mind, even though I had not yet then experienced the deaths I have experienced since, though I had experienced some deaths that mattered greatly to me. The idea came into my mind that one might be dead, and the door shut forever—forever! what a thing to accept!—between oneself and the living, and yet, somehow, one might still hear an occasional echo from the world of the living, an echo of what one sometimes used to hear. And it may be true that we can still hear things after death that we heard in life. We don't know—though I don't really believe we continue to hear things from the world of the living. But I don't know.

Another thing that came my way by chance, some weeks ago, and added itself to the things that enter my life and ideas borne merely—as it seems—by the passing stream of time, was a poem most likely by Walter Raleigh.

We, in my book group, were talking about a poem by John Ashbery called "As You Came from the Holy Land." This title, one of us said, reminded him of an earlier poem of the same title by someone else. He knew it was centuries earlier but he couldn't remember who wrote it. We looked it up and it turned out to be a poem attributed to Walter Raleigh, written in the sixteenth or early seventeenth century. So far away in time, poets so unlike. Curious. But clearly, we thought, Ashbery must have modeled his poem on the Raleigh poem. We thought this not only because of the title but also because of another feature they share: the way, in the first lines, the holy land is identified not as Jerusalem, for instance, but somewhere much more local to the writer.

The Raleigh poem repeats the title in the first line and then goes on in the second to identify the holy land that he has in mind, and follows with some questions:

AS YOU CAME FROM
THE HOLY LAND

As you came from the holy land
of Walsingham,
Met you not with my true love
By the way as you came?

As I read the poem, which I did not know before, I am taken by the language and my interest in Raleigh is piqued. The repetition of "as you came" strikes me as being pleasingly awkward, in the same way as the title "Peter and Mother" — its awkwardness and pleasingness being the reason I think of it so often. You shouldn't do that, but you can absolutely do that!

Walsingham, in Norfolk, was one of the great Christian pilgrimage destinations at the time, I have learned, but it comes with a chime of the prosaic after the implied Middle Eastern grandeur of "holy land," especially in our day, when most of us are not aware that Walsingham was a place of pilgrimage.

Ashbery, exceptionally for him in the book we are reading, has the first sentence of the poem begin with the title. And what he identifies as the holy land is holy only for him; it was never a traditional Christian destination:

AS YOU CAME FROM
THE HOLY LAND

of western New York State

Now he, too, goes on to ask questions, the Raleigh poem having perhaps established the pattern for this one:

were the graves all right in their bushings
was there a note of panic in the late
    Autumn air
because the old man had peed in his
    pants again
was there turning away from the late
    afternoon glare
as though it too could be wished away
was any of this present . . .

Western New York State, specifically the Rochester area, was Ashbery's birthplace and where he spent his childhood and youth; here, as he describes, he was happier when living in his grandparents' "gloomy but cozy" house than his parents' farmhouse, in which he was vulnerable to his father's unpredictable "explosive temper" and physical violence.

The Raleigh poem is in the form of a dialogue that could be summarized as follows, with scraps of quotations from particularly nice bits of repetition: As you came from Walsingham, did you encounter my true love? How would I know her? You'd know her because "There is none hath a form so divine / In the earth, or the air." I did meet someone like that, "Who like a queen, like a nymph, did appear / By her gait, by her grace." She has left me all alone, though she used to love me. Why has she left you, having once loved you? Because I'm old now: "Love likes not the falling fruit from the withered tree." Love is careless, blind and deaf, and never faithful: "His desire is a dureless content," whereas "True love is a durable fire."

I am enjoying this exploration of the poem, with its language so different from Ashbery's yet inspiring to Ashbery. When I look up "dureless," I find an illustrative quotation in Samuel Johnson's dictionary, but nothing in Webster's. The quotation I find is in fact from Raleigh, but not from this poem, rather from a four-volume work called *The History of the World,* which he wrote while confined in the Tower of London. He was there from 1603 to 1616; then released to go on an expedition; then returned to the Tower until his execution in 1618, having had many years of enforced leisure there. The man of action and adventure was there forced to sit still.

Raleigh was that unusual combination — a writer very much living the productive life of the intellect, but also a daring adventurer who periodically exposed himself to great physical danger. He lived to be old by the standards of the day—sixty-six—and would have lived longer had he not been put to death. And despite the lines of his poem, which was evidently not autobiographical, his true love and wife, Bess Throgmorton, remained faithful to him. She was also imprisoned in the Tower, and it was there that the second of their two surviving children was both conceived and born. After Raleigh was beheaded, his embalmed head was given to his widow, who kept it till her death.

As for Ashbery, his adventures were mostly intellectual, aesthetic, linguistic, inter-lingual, formal, cosmopolitan, and with a lower degree of physical risk, though surely some—as far as I know. He lived to what is now considered an advanced age—ninety—having continued to teach for many years. He, too, like Raleigh, enjoyed what appeared to be a continuing faithful love, even as a withered tree.

Melville, like Raleigh, invited physical risk, in his youth, and experienced high adventure, including what would have been the gruesome subject of a certain type of comic book I can imagine being relished by

Ashbery as a boy—he was captured on a tropical island and held prisoner for nearly four weeks by a tribe of cannibals. He might have been eaten, but he was not, instead being rescued by an Australian whaler. By the time he was twenty-five, his adventuring was over, and he settled down to write first *Typee*—whose protagonist endures not four weeks but four months with the cannibals—and then *Omoo,* and after several more shorter novels in quick succession, his vastly ambitious but less enthusiastically received "mighty" novel, *Moby-Dick.*

When I am asked why I write and instead think about how I write, the following occurs to me: in a longer project, one that extends over time, like the writing of this essay—and even, on a smaller scale, in a shorter project—there is sometimes, if I am receptive and circumstances allow it, a productive interaction between the active writing and the intervals away from active writing. The active writing produces new ideas, which get put into words on the page. Then, during the time away from writing, my brain continues its associations, continues to produce afterthoughts. And if I write these down, usually hastily, in the midst of other tasks, then I have notes to carry back to the desk, and these notes then provide a starting point for the active writing, in case I don't have one ready already, which I often don't. So this circular motion continues productively, one activity generating the other in a closed system.

After I had been reading this last paragraph over yesterday (and before I wrote what I am in the midst of writing now), I found myself talking about it, since it was on my mind, with a nurseryman of my acquaintance in a plant nursery on a sunny hilltop twenty minutes from here — the nursery being deserted by other customers, since it is now late October and the desire to acquire more plants has diminished in most people around here, though not in me. I had selected and paid for seven smooth asters and two mountain mints — threadleaf — and they were sitting on a cart waiting for us to trundle them to my car. The nurseryman agreed that one can continue thinking about a project while doing physical work and that he does a lot of thinking especially while watering his stock. I continued to think about this conversation as I drove home through the woods, the plants swaying in the back, as I could see in the rearview mirror, down a long wooded road twice crossed by small tribes of turkeys, the road so little traveled that I saw not a single other car on my way home and stopped once, in the middle of the road, for as long as I wanted, to watch the turkeys as they picked their way into the woods. My previous conversation with the nurseryman, on a visit when the nursery had again been deserted and I had again bought some mountain mint—again threadleaf—had been one with a doomsday theme. He expressed his sadness that in such a beautiful world, in which we are given so much that is positive, there is so much conflict and strife, and I agreed.

I have these days also, after decades, been rereading Hamsun's *Hunger,* having at first opened the book again in search of the building, originally a pharmacy, then a restaurant called the Pharmacy, where my friend and I might have had dinner, where we had planned to have dinner, a building that sat up against a steep hillside, had a center entryway and two sections, right and left, the left-hand part being where we wanted to eat, and the right-hand part being, I seemed to remember, a large bar with wood paneling and thick wooden tables— remembered mistakenly, it turns out, as I discovered when I asked a Norwegian friend. No, it was not a bar but another, humbler, restaurant.

The novel is more various and lively this time than I remembered. It had stayed in my mind, all these years, as forceful and unusual but a grim and repetitive account of hunger never satisfied, of the protagonist Knut's insane strategies for surviving and especially for appeasing his hunger, such as by sucking on a splinter of wood. I had remembered it as little more than this account of desperate hunger, but now I see how Hamsun returns to the basic theme and material for page after page without losing variety and liveliness, partly because of Knut's vivid, insane thoughts and behaviors, his impassioned convictions, the confidence in his tone as he narrates his bleak and bizarre story. This feat Hamsun pulls off is not completely unlike the feat of J. A. Baker, with his very different subject and mood, as with a limited set of elements he maintains the variation, and even drama, of his estuary and its populations on page after page.

The irrational behavior of Hamsun's protagonist as he describes it himself—in the first person—has reminded me unexpectedly of the young mother in Elena Ferrante's *Days of Abandonment,* who also behaves at times in a way that we would call insane. But in the case of both these novels, because the story is told in the first person, from within the point of view of the at times wildly erratic protagonist—because we are borne along within a highly individual system of logic from one seemingly reasonable action to the next—we do not always see this mad behavior for what it is. Only if we step back for a moment do we measure it against more conventional behavior. Simply through the use of first-person narration rather than third, we are persuaded, at least intermittently, that for every wild move of the protagonist, there is a sound motive.

Part of the day in which I am writing this is a day of high wind that gusts, as they promised, to even stronger winds. It is also a day of tornado warnings, and when I was outdoors earlier, working in the yard despite some risk, I watched the horizon for a dark funnel. Indoors now, I keep saving my work on the computer against a different risk—the loss of some text. The warnings today have been for high winds and tornadoes, but also floods. After a while, now, the wind dies down. It has risen and gusted, as promised, and now that is over. But coming up soon may be heavy rains and floods.

On a Saturday morning not long after the days of wind and rain, I happen to read a poem of John Clare's that comes via a regular Saturday morning missive. The commentary attached to the poem reminds me of things I already know about him: that John Clare walked eighty miles from his asylum to his home and family, and that he wrote a prose account of this journey addressed to his fictional wife, Mary Clare — the woman he wished he had been allowed to marry. It was the account of a long journey on foot in which he endured hunger and exhaustion, by a man no longer young but whom I tend to think of, illogically, as young, perhaps only because of the simplicity of his name and the fact that he lived and wrote several hundred years before our time — does earlier make him younger? — or because I often read the poems he wrote when he was young. Clare was incarcerated for twenty-seven years in an apparently laxly or casually or permissibly guarded "madhouse" in Essex and, being in the habit of taking long walks in the surrounding forests, he had one day wandered north to return home, arriving at his destination after several days of walking. Clare, too, was concerned about his footwear — one shoe had nearly lost its sole.

What the commentary on Saturday morning did not say, but what I knew, was that along the way he had little to eat and became very hungry: "I sat down half an hour and made a good many wishes for breakfast, but wishes was no hearty meal." A few pages later he writes: "On the third day I satisfied my hunger by eating the grass by the roadside, which seemed to taste something like bread. I was hungry and ate heartily till I was satisfied and in fact the meal seemed to do me good."

This reminded me, of course, of Knut Hamsun's character chewing on splinters of wood.

And then, recently, I read *Love, Joe,* a selection of letters by Joe Brainard, who described living on so little money, in Boston, at the age of nineteen, that for eight days he had nothing to eat each day but a little bread. But Brainard chose not to work at a job, in order to spend his time on his art — his painting and collages. And Hamsun's protagonist, too, chose not to get a job, although he tried to earn money, and sometimes succeeded, by composing essays, even under great difficulty, once standing out on the street and writing with a pencil by the light from a streetlamp when he had no light in his room, and trying to place them in a local newspaper, for which he would be paid 10 kroner. John Clare, walking away from the asylum, also chose to go without food. So these particular cases of desperate hunger were in fact brought about through some degree of choice, though in the case of true insanity, if Clare's was true insanity, it may be debatable how much of any sort of choice he had, and in the case of a work of fiction, one can fabricate anything, though Hamsun was apparently basing the novel on his own experiences. (And then I am reminded, further, of the fictional Harriet in Brand's *The Outward Room* who, having no money left after she pawned her brother's ring, goes hungry for several days until a stranger, who will soon become a close companion, buys her a cup of coffee.)

The character Knut sucking on a splinter of wood reminds me of another fictional character, Beckett's Molloy, sucking one by one on sixteen pebbles that he moves in a set order, several times reconsidered, from pocket to pocket—the action narrated in such painstaking detail that this, too, may be an example of a passage bordering on the tedious.

Knut Hamsun began writing *Hunger* in 1888, when he was twenty-nine years old. It was apparently based on his own struggles with pennilessness, hunger, and fruitless searches for work, but he condensed ten years of those experiences into a few months (as Melville, in contrary motion, expanded his actual four weeks with the cannibals into four months in his novel). As I read along in it, not just picturing this young man but rather living empathically through his struggles, the experience began to remind me of the other accounts of physical hardship I had been living through empathically, these closer to the autobiographical truth. I saw that I was collapsing, or associating, several figures in several accounts: the young protagonist of *Hunger*; the very elderly author Hamsun, many decades later, judged insane by some, walking for such long hours away from and back to the home for the aged; and John Clare the poet walking north to his (real) wife and children.

The poetry of John Clare was another choice of my book group, which was why I happened to read, besides our chosen poems, his prose account of his "escape" from the lunatic asylum. Clare, as it happened, was one of the six "certifiably minor" poets that Ashbery discussed in *Other Traditions*.

Another person, another writer, I now associate with John Clare and Hamsun's character (himself) in *On Overgrown Paths,* is Robert Walser. I'm surprised the parallel hadn't occurred to me until now, in October, after all these months in which Hamsun and Clare were so present in my mind. For the last twenty-seven years of his life, Walser was also confined to a mental institution — apparently by preference, at least in part, in some unacknowledged way. Admitted to one asylum and then a second, sleeping by choice in a communal dormitory room, he continued to write for a time — in barely decipherable micro-script — but he also did manual work there, like the other patients. One task he had was to glue paper bags together, and another was to sort and unravel twine for the post office. But he was "content" with this work. He, too, like Clare, was permitted to go out on his own and take walks. Another book composed of intermittent chronological entries is Carl Seelig's *Walks with Walser,* translated by Anne Posten, about the occasions on which he, who was Walser's editor and executor as well as friend, would join Walser, usually meeting him at a railway station, and set off on a long walk, stopping at an inn or tavern along the way to have something to eat and drink. Seelig recounts their conversations, and also what they ate and drank (vermouth and hot cheese pie; or Bernese rösti, fried eggs, and meringues; some glasses of lager . . .). Walser's last walk was by himself. Not far from the asylum, on Christmas Day, he was found lying dead in the snow, a tall man, his arm flung over his head, his hat a few feet away.

A late discovery, made by chance. The title "Peter and Mother" is not that of an Ashbery poem after all, or an article about Ashbery, but of a poem by David Schubert that Ashbery quotes in his last Norton essay — on David Schubert — that includes the lines:

> At evening the door opened on clematis
> And his mother with a shawl ran down the
>   years
> To meet someone with an empty lunch-box.

(The name Peter is not mentioned in the poem.)

I will end with this.

I wrote another story about death that developed more slowly and with more difficulty, starting from some confusing thoughts about what is lost when someone dies who has a rich mind and a complex and nuanced sensibility.

When I decided that I could try to answer the question of why I write by looking at why I write certain stories, I saw that, like the tedious woman in my story "The Foundation," I write also, sometimes, to figure out something I don't understand. That material outside me, or inside me but coming to me as though found in a field, in this case as a sudden perception, does more than just "bother" me, as something to which I want to give a form. It is something I don't fully understand and that I want to understand. A story may then evolve from that. Perhaps I think that putting a thought into a formal piece of writing may help me understand a puzzle.

The puzzle started with the death of a woman I did not know very well. It was the very fact that I did not know her well that caused me to have these thoughts — since they were not complicated by any long or deep attachment to her.

She was an elderly friend of the elderly mother of a friend of mine in my village. I had first met her at a one-time local gathering, long in the organizing, called the Jewish Farmers Reunion, which she attended because her family had had a chicken farm on the outskirts of our village. My friend and I attended because we were interested in all things having to do with local history.

The second time I saw her was when the four of us had dinner together one night at the residence where she and my friend's mother lived, across the river in an upscale assisted living place with tablecloths, waitstaff, and wine. I enjoyed the dinner and the company and looked forward to more dinners, to crossing the river again in my friend's car to see the two old women. I decided I would regard my new acquaintance as a sort of youthful aunt, with her sense of humor, her gentleness, her sharpness and poise, her fund of memories of the old days in the village.

Then, within months of that night, she fell seriously ill with a condition that would require painful and protracted treatment. She chose instead to refuse treatment and just let herself go. She was gone within weeks. I felt the loss personally, but I also perceived what a loss of an enriched mind her death was. That mind of hers, which had developed over a lifetime to what it was — through her childhood on the farm, her young womanhood, her marriage and motherhood, her maturity, and the rich and lively friendships of old age — to become as complex and surprising as it now was, was now shut down, gone forever in a moment, at her death.

In my thoughts I went beyond the moment of her death. I thought about how, physically, her brain cells — the source of her memories, her wit — would begin to soften and lose their elasticity as soon as the blood ceased to flow around them. And about how the parts of her brain, specifically, that contained the memories of my village would soften and collapse — quite quickly.

There was sadness but also amazement, for me, in thinking about all this. The same wonder we return to habitually whenever we recognize that our apparently disembodied thoughts are not disembodied but quite physically located somewhere within our brains — we even know the approximate locations — shooting around as electrical impulses.

And then I associated these thoughts with what went on in my own brain, which still had blood flowing through it, and electricity, including my constant attempts, all my life, to improve my German — for no particular reason! The German in my brain was better now than it had been in my twenties, or my forties. The thought of those constant efforts, which seemed to me funny and a little pathetic, now came together with my thoughts about the end of my elderly friend, which had not been funny.

There was a third element at the origin of this little story. The story had a model, a poem I have read for decades now, an untitled folk poem translated by the poet Anselm Hollo from the Cheremis language. I had read it repeatedly because—in the same sense as Ashbery's experience with the painting by Parmigianino—this poem had "bothered" me for a long time. It puzzled me because it was a piece of writing that had continued to have the same surprising impact on me though I knew it so well. How did it do that? It is only three lines long.

> I shouldn't have started these red wool
> mittens.
> they're done now,
> but my life is over.

What a small poem. But as with other short and simple pieces of writing, and long and complex ones too, there is the surface sense of it and then more beneath the surface—in this case, the fact that whatever our projects may be, life comes to an end, we come to an end. Or that our projects consume our life, and then we die. Or that we spend our life on activities that may turn out to have used up our life pointlessly.

This poem gave me a pattern for the beginning of my story, but then my story continued in a slightly different direction:

IMPROVING MY GERMAN

All my life I have been trying to improve my
    German.
At last my German is better!
But now I am old and ill.
I will die soon.
But when they take me to my grave,
I will have,
somewhere in my brain,
better German.

So all that pondering, and trying to accept or articulate something I had not fully comprehended before, resulted in a very short story with the broken lines of a poem, a very short story that nevertheless had a lot of thinking behind it, and then a lot of revision to arrive at it, and an upcropping within it of the humor that I perceived in my own relationship to German but that did not exist in the original situation that so struck me and led me to thoughts my only initial response to which seemed useless — saying to myself, of the loss of my friend's mind, What a waste!

Giving form to an aspect of my puzzlement and sadness, even though I did not mention my friend or her death, helped to relieve my feelings by transmuting them into the solidity of a piece of writing. It relieved me, too, of my amusement at my attempts to learn German — for amusement, too, likes to be relieved. So it must be that relieving myself of the burdens of strong feelings, by taking them out of myself and putting them into an objective form, a form that can also be shared by others out in the world, is yet another reason why I write.